This book belongs to

_____

365 DAYS OF Prayer FOR MOTHERS

BroadStreet
PUBLISHING

BroadStreet Publishing Group LLC
Savage, Minnesota, USA
Broadstreetpublishing.com

365 Days of Prayer for Mothers

© 2020 BroadStreet Publishing

978-1-4245-5817-9
978-1-4245-5818-6 (ebook)

Prayers composed by Stephanie Sample and Michelle Winger.

Design by Chris Garborg | garborgdesign.com
Compiled and edited by Michelle Winger | literallyprecise.com

Printed in China.

20 21 22 23 24 25   6 5 4 3 2 1

"Come to me, all of you who are weary and carry heavy burdens, and I will give you rest."

Matthew 11:28 NLT

Introduction

Whether you've been a person of prayer for many years or this is your first prayer devotional, we hope you are blessed and inspired by the daily prayers written here. Ultimately, prayer is a conversation with God. You don't need to use fancy words or recite long passages of Scripture. Just talk to God. Open your heart. He adores you, and he's listening to every word you say.

Some days your prayers may be filled with gratitude, some days with repentance, and some with need. Just lay your heart and your prayers at the Father's feet and wait for his powerful response.

May God bless you as you connect daily with him.

As you develop a habit of prayer, think about this:

Praise

Begin by telling God how wonderful he is. Focus on which of his many attributes you are grateful for.

Repentance

Before you present your needs to God, pause. Take a moment to examine your heart. If God reveals any unconfessed sin, bring it before him and ask for forgiveness.

Ask

What do you need from your Father in heaven today? Ask him boldly; he is waiting to grant you the desires of your heart.

Yield

Ask as if it will be done, and yield to his will. Acknowledge he may know something you don't or have something even better in mind for you. Trust and accept whatever answer you receive.

January

The earnest prayer of a
righteous person has great power
and produces wonderful results.

JAMES 5:16 NLT

Your Plan Is Perfect

Many are the plans in a person's heart,
but it is the LORD's purpose that prevails.
PROVERBS 19:21 NIV

God, as I sit here imagining the coming year, I can't help but reflect on the last one. I think of the plans I made, and I see your fingerprints on every memory like the fingerprints my children leave on windows and mirrors. Thank you for knowing what I truly need, regardless of what I might plan. Every time I succeeded—and each time I failed—you were right there keeping me safe and pointing me to you. Forgive the selfish ambitions and poor choices of last year, and plant in me a desire to do your will, to want what you want for myself and for my children. Your plan for our lives is perfect; let me remember that as I consider the coming year.

What would you like to see change this year?

Choosing Well

Trust in the LORD with all your heart,
And lean not on your own understanding;
In all your ways acknowledge Him,
And He shall direct your paths.
PROVERBS 3:5-6 NKJV

God, you are completely faithful, and I trust you with my life. Every decision matters to you: from the words I say and the food I eat, to where I live or send my children to school. Even though I sometimes choose selfishly—what would be easy, stress-free, or fun—you always forgive me. You chose to send your perfect Son, Jesus, to pay for my sins; how can I doubt that you'll hear my prayers and lead me to the best decisions? Guide me now, Father, to choose well how to spend this moment, this day with my children, this life.

Are you ready to trust God completely with your life and the life of your children?

This Work Matters

Whatever you do, work heartily,
as for the Lord and not for men.
COLOSSIANS 3:23 ESV

God, I know your ways are perfect and that you placed me exactly where I am for a reason. There are moments though, that my life seems like endless drudgery. How can this kind of work matter? These dishes, the snowy sidewalks, the diapers, the homework assignments. Help me remember all I do is for you. Let me clear the sidewalk as if you were about to walk on it—to wash the dishes as if you were going to eat from them. Give me a glimpse, when I need it, of the many thankless tasks you've done for me, and the energy to do the job before me as if for you.

What is your reason for doing all your tasks?

A Positive Influence

> "Let your light shine before men in such a way
> that they may see your good works, and glorify
> your Father who is in heaven."
> MATTHEW 5:16 NASB

Jesus, thank you for your perfect example of how to live in the light. Your goodness inspires me to be a positive influence in my home with my children, and in my community. Sometimes I forget this and behave in ways that don't reflect your beauty and brilliance, and I'm sorry for that, Lord. Help me remember to keep my lamp on a stand, burning brightly, and encourage my children to do the same. Let me live in a way that draws them to you. Let them see me and hear me and know that I am yours. Let my life bring you glory!

How will your light shine before those in your path today?

Please Send Friends

If either of them falls down,
one can help the other up.
But pity anyone who falls
and has no one to help them up.
ECCLESIASTES 4:10 NIV

God, you are such a faithful friend! No one could care more about me than you do. I know you designed us for relationships, and I do long to be around people—especially people who love you. I thank you for the children you've given me: little people to give a hand to and to get a hand from, and I ask your forgiveness for the days I don't appreciate them as I should. I ask you, Lord, to continue enriching my life with friends as well. Lead me into relationships that stretch me as I see other ways to live, to love, and to pour into one another.

How can you be a faithful friend both to your children and to those special people in your life?

Brought Low

The righteous cry out, and the LORD hears,
And delivers them out of all their troubles.
PSALM 34:17 NKJV

Father, there are days I just want to crawl into your lap and stay, like my children sometimes want to do with me. When those days string together and I find myself brought low, it comforts me to know you see my sadness and you want nothing more than to take it from me. You don't consider me ungrateful or selfish on these days; you just love me. Thank you for the shelter of your arms, the comfort of your embrace, and the deliverance of your perfect love. Hold me close today, Abba Father. Hear my cries and remind me what it means to be your dearly beloved child. Help me to be a comfort to my children when they are feeling low too.

Do you need to be held close today by your Abba Father?

Abide in Me

"Abide in me, and I in you. As the branch cannot
bear fruit by itself, unless it abides in the vine,
neither can you, unless you abide in me."
JOHN 15:4 ESV

Lord Jesus, I can't understand why I sometimes try to do things apart from you. Only bitter, unripe fruit comes from those efforts, yet I seem to forget this, and I plough ahead with all my chores and errands. But you always forgive me. You are so patient with me as I struggle to make my own way, knowing full well that to abide in you is the only way. Jesus, keep me close! Remind me how much I need you when I start to think I can do all these tasks on my own. The fruit that comes from a life with you is the sweetest taste I've known, and it's the only way I want to live.

Are you abiding in God to help you get through each day with its endless chores and errands?

Fully Committed

"Devote yourselves completely to the LORD our God, walking
in his statutes and keeping his commandments,
as at this day."
1 KINGS 8:61 NRSV

Lord, I belong to you. I adore you, and I want to
live my life fully committed to you. I realize there are
days—maybe more than not—when I don't behave
as though this were true, but that is not what is in
my heart. Knowing Jesus laid down his perfect life
for me, I want only to honor his sacrifice by doing
the same. Because I am weak, I know that even
though I want this, I can't do it without your help.
Strengthen me, God, to live my life for you. Help
me to show my children what it looks like to live
surrendered to you—to give you everything I am and
all that I have. I want them to know what it looks like
to be fully committed and devoted to you.

**How can you be completely devoted to the Lord in this
season of life?**

Deliver Me

"Lead us not into temptation,
but deliver us from the evil one."
MATTHEW 6:13 NIV

Lord, there is so much evil in this world. Every day a new danger, disaster, or form of depravity conspires to lure me from the peace of a life lived with you. It's tempting to give in—to worry, to fear, even to my own pleasure—and sometimes I do. But this is not your way, and yours is the only way I want to live. So please forgive me. Forgive and deliver me, God, from the evil sights, sounds, and thoughts that bombard my senses. Help me to know that you hold me and my children in your hand. Deliver me to your perfect peace, that place where none of it can touch me or my family.

Are you ready to be delivered into God's perfect peace?

Hold Me Accountable

Each of us shall give account of himself to God.
ROMANS 14:12 NKJV

Lord, I recognize your authority over all. I know that if I were to give account of myself today—my thoughts and actions— and compare it to the wonderful plans you have for my life, I'd come up short. You would forgive me and welcome me as your child, but I would know I could have done so much more to honor you and build the kingdom. Hold me accountable, Father! Hold me to your high standards, and plant in me a desire and a drive to meet them so that when I meet you face-to-face, I'll know you are well pleased with me.

How do you find ways to be accountable?

So Much Grace

From his fullness we have all received, grace upon grace.
JOHN 1:16 NRSV

God, how do I begin to thank you for your grace? By definition I am unworthy, and daily I prove this to be true. Every poor decision, every impatient word, every sin—large or small—magnifies your grace until it's so immense, it's all I can see. Impossibly, you love me no matter what I do. I don't even have to ask; I think that's what amazes me most of all. Before I even know I need it, it's already given. Freely, gratuitously, wonderfully, you lavish me with your love and forgiveness. How wholly inadequate are the thanks I offer in return, yet what else can I do? I thank you again for your grace and ask you to help me extend the same grace to those you have lovingly placed in my care.

Have you thanked God for his grace lately?

Loneliness

Even if my father and mother abandon me,
the LORD will hold me close.
PSALM 27:10 NLT

How amazing it is to remember I am never alone! You, Holy Spirit, are my constant companion. You are always here to help, guide, and comfort me. How I feel alone when my children are nearby seems absurd, but it's real. Whether I'm truly by myself or simply somewhere the conversation doesn't penetrate my heart, I find myself aching for connection and coming up empty. Forgive me for forgetting you are there, Spirit of God. Please remind me that loneliness is a gift designed to point me to you. Only you can take away the ache of aloneness, Lord. The closer I am walking with you, the fuller my life becomes—regardless of who is with me.

How do you feel knowing that you are never alone?

Refresh and Restore

It is in vain that you rise up early
and go late to rest,
eating the bread of anxious toil;
for he gives to his beloved sleep.
PSALM 127:2 ESV

God who never sleeps, I am in awe. Sometimes I try to trade places with you, working as if I need no rest and determined to meet everyone's every need. And there you are, tireless, ready to catch me as I collapse from the effort of it all. Thank you for your endless effort on my behalf. You designed us for times of great accomplishment—and times of replenishment. Remind me that I need rest and reassure me it's okay to take it, Lord. Refresh and restore me as I break from all my striving and help me remember that even in the light of my best effort, it is you who truly provides.

Do you need God's rest and refreshment today?

A Heart That Would

I plead with you to give your bodies to God because
of all he has done for you. Let them be a living and
holy sacrifice—the kind he will find acceptable.
This is truly the way to worship him.

ROMANS 12:1 NLT

Father, I want to thank you today for the people, living and past, who have sacrificed on behalf of me and my family. When I consider all the public servants who daily risk their lives, so we can live safe and free, my gratitude overwhelms me. Would I step into harm's way for them? I am aware that people I will never know sacrificed their wages, their time, and their talents so I can seek and connect with you freely. Would I sacrifice my resources to ensure the next generation will find you here? Create in me a heart that would, God. Willingly, joyfully, and filled with gratitude, give me a heart that would.

Do you have a heart that would?

Accepting Others

As it is in your heart, let it be in mine.
Christ accepted you, so you should accept each other,
which will bring glory to God.
ROMANS 15:7 NCV

Like the perfect Father you are, you accept me as I am. Why, then, is it so hard for me to accept others? It seems so easy to find fault, cast blame, and criticize, unfortunately even with the children you have blessed me with, but this is not what you want. This does not bring you glory. When I imagine Jesus picking and choosing who is "worthy" of his acceptance the way I sometimes do, I am filled with remorse. Who am I to decide who is worthy when you have already decided: all are worthy. All are welcome. Thank you.

Did you feel worthy today? Did you make those in your care feel worthy?

Run to Win

Do you not know that in a race all the runners run,
but only one gets the prize? Run in such a way
as to get the prize.
1 CORINTHIANS 9:24 NIV

Lord, when I think of Jesus' incredible humility, how every moment in his life was one in which he could have easily "won," I can scarcely comprehend it. I like to win; I also like to be right. Will you help me to discern when these desires are appropriate, and when I need reigning in? When there is a prize worth having at stake—when you want me to run to win— please give me the strength, courage, and ambition to give it everything I've got to win the crown. And when the so-called prize comes at the expense of a relationship, or when it simply doesn't matter, nudge me, Lord, to prefer others and slow it to a jog.

Are you running to win the ultimate prize?

Forgiven

> "Whenever you stand praying, forgive,
> if you have anything against anyone;
> so that your Father in heaven may also
> forgive you your trespasses."
> MARK 11:25 NRSV

Sinless, perfect Lord, you've forgiven every wrong I've ever committed, along with those sins still to come. No wonder you ask that before I ask for anything for myself, I forgive those who have wronged me. With a heart so open to forgiveness, how it must grieve you when I hold onto a grudge or nurse my anger. Will you help me? Show me where bitterness has taken hold; inspire me to reach out in love and reconciliation and mend every relationship that's been broken due to an old hurt. This is all I ask of you in this moment: help me forgive, that I may be forgiven.

What unforgiveness might be lurking in your heart?

Gifts in Disguise

Give thanks in all circumstances;
for this is the will of God in Christ Jesus for you.
1 THESSALONIANS 5:18 ESV

God, there is no end to your gifts. From the breath in my lungs, to the roof over my head, to the children who surround me, every small mercy is a gift from you. Thank you so much, Father, for the attention you pay to me. When things like a vacated nap or a broadcast interruption during my child's favorite show send me into a fit of grumbling, thank you also for your patience. Those moments are chances to connect with you, to read your Word, to give you thanks. They are gifts disguised as inconveniences. In every circumstance, I thank you.

In what circumstance do you need to be thankful?

Inspire Me

God created great sea creatures and every living thing
that scurries and swarms in the water, and every sort of bird—
each producing offspring of the same kind.
And God saw that it was good.
GENESIS 1:21 NLT

Wonderful, God, everywhere I look I see signs of your inventiveness, your playfulness, and your creativity. How did you create these children with different tastes, appearances, and temperaments? I take this beautiful world for granted when I should be using it for inspiration. God, will you inspire me today? Give me a fresh idea, a new perspective, an infusion of passion so that my work in this home and outside of it will be a delight to us both. Lift me out of my rut, Lord, and tilt my chin upward to the dozen shades of blue in the sky. Inspire me, God, and then send me off to inspire others.

How are you inspired by God today?

No Compromise

"If you love me, obey my commandments."
JOHN 14:15 NLT

Jesus, I love you. How can I not, when you have done so much for me and my children, and you ask so little in return? You want me to love you and to prove it by loving others. Each time I pass up an opportunity to help, to forgive, to sacrifice, I compromise my love for you. This is not how I want to live! Help me, Holy Spirit, through temptation. Remind me of the love I have in and for Jesus and let that bind me to make choices that honor that love. Like a child who wants to please a parent, let me choose to please you.

How can you please Jesus today?

I'm Weary

Those who wait for the Lord shall renew their strength,
they shall mount up with wings like eagles,
they shall run and not be weary,
they shall walk and not faint.

ISAIAH 40:31 NRSV

Lord, your power knows no limits. When I think of how boundless your strength, how endless your ability, I stand in awe. Considering how easily I tire with the daily tasks of the house, and how quickly I become overwhelmed by the small people in my house, it is clear I am not calling upon your power enough. I'm weary, Father. Responsibilities mount and threaten to overwhelm me. Instead of giving in and lying down, I call upon your supernatural power. Infuse me, Lord! Spring up a well of energy in this empty vessel. With your help, exhaustion will not win. Allow me to finish strong so I can shout of your provision to all who can hear.

How have you experienced God's supernatural power?

Season of Grief

Since we believe that Jesus died and rose again,
even so, through Jesus, God will bring with him
those who have fallen asleep.
1 THESSALONIANS 4:14 ESV

God in heaven, today is one of those days I wish I were there. I miss the people who have gone before me. Though I know I will be reunited one day with all who knew you and loved you, sometimes I can't help wishing I didn't have to wait. A familiar scent, a laugh or gesture from a passing stranger, and it all comes back: the longing, the aching for the way it used to be. Let me feel your presence today, Lord. Let me experience your comfort. Let the memories make me smile, and the promise of future days cause me to rejoice. I trust your timing, and I rest in your promise because grief will pass.

When have you most felt God's comfort?

Loving Well

"A new commandment I give to you,
that you love one another, even as I have loved you,
that you also love one another."
JOHN 13:34 NASB

Nothing is more amazing than your love, Father. The depth is so vast, I get lost in it—and what could be better? From this place, swimming in your love, it is easy to love others. Then, reality hits. All it takes is an ill-timed interruption by a small voice, or an unintended slight caused by a complaint, and I find myself out of the ocean, wallowing in a puddle of self-righteousness. Help me to love as you love, Jesus! Deeply, without hesitation or thought of self. I know this is what you ask of me—how you will know that I love you—yet still I struggle. Pull me from my puddle as often as you must; plunge me into the sea of your love again and again, so that I may love as you do.

Have you experienced God's love for others recently?

Casting My Burden

Cast your burden on the LORD,
And He shall sustain you;
He shall never permit the righteous to be moved.
PSALM 55:22 NKJV

God, how strong your arms must be! How sturdy your back, to carry the burdens of all who are wise enough to hand them over. I sometimes hold onto my sadness as though I need it survive. Why do I do that? It's heavy, and my arms ache from the weight. Can I give it to you? I ask not because I'm not sure if you are willing, but because I'm not sure I'm strong enough. Will you pry open my aching arms and remove it from my chest when I cannot? Then will you stay with me, holding me up as I learn to balance without it?

How will you let God carry your burden?

Mercy upon Mercy

"They are blessed who show mercy to others,
for God will show mercy to them."
MATTHEW 5:7 NCV

Merciful God, your compassion astonishes me. You show me how to live by how you love, and you love with such mercy it moves me to tears. How can it be that a heart so strong is also so tender? Every morning you wipe the slate clean, just because you love us. How can I give that back? How can I show my children the same kind of mercy that you show me? I cannot, though I wish to keep trying. Every merciful act on my part comes back to me multiplied. That's so like you, piling mercy upon mercy, grace upon grace, gift upon gift. How can I thank you, but to grow in mercy myself?

Did you sense God's mercy today for yourself or others?

Quick to Listen

Take note of this: Everyone should be quick to listen,
slow to speak and slow to become angry.

JAMES 1:19 NIV

Lord, you are the great listener. You hear every cry;
you answer every call. Your attentiveness to me
inspires me to be more attentive to the children you
have blessed me with, yet invariably I find myself not
listening, just smiling and nodding my head, though
I've scarcely taken in a word. Let me be quick to
listen, God! When my children feel safe enough with
me to open themselves up, move me instantly to sink
back and take it in. Let me see these interactions
as invitations into their hearts, not opportunities to
dispense my thoughts. Move me to ask questions, to
draw them out further, and when I do speak, let my
words be chosen by you.

Are you a good listener?

Forever Gifts

God's gifts and his call can never be withdrawn.
ROMANS 11:29 NLT

God, giver of good gifts, once you called me to you and I responded, those gifts began to flow. I felt you, I heard you, and your power surged in me in new and wonderful ways. You also gave me some challenges. I know everything you've given me has been for good—for my own or my family's, or for your church, but I confess that sometimes I question your choices. I wander back to old habits and fall into old ways, and it's hard to hear your voice or feel your presence. Your power feels distant; did I imagine it? These are the times I cling to the knowledge that I cannot lose you, and just like that, the clinging brings me back where I belong.

How do you see God's gifts flowing in you and out to your children?

While I Wait

Be strong, and let your heart take courage,
all you who wait for the LORD!
PSALM 31:24 ESV

God, waiting is hard! I look for the shortest lines in the grocery store and the quickest-moving lane of traffic, and then I come to you and request the timeliest solutions to all my problems. My family needs clothes, there's no food for lunches, and the children have taken to arguing…again. When you don't answer right away, doubt creeps in. Are you listening? Are you there? I need your encouragement, Lord, as I wait for your perfect resolution. Help me remember that you see the big picture, and that your plan is for the best possible outcome, which is not necessarily the quickest. Fortify my heart with patience, courage, and strength while I wait. I trust your plan, and I rejoice in knowing all will be well.

Do you have trouble waiting for the Lord?

Every Good Thing

Every good thing given and every perfect gift is from above,
coming down from the Father of lights, with whom
there is no variation or shifting shadow.
JAMES 1:17 NASB

Lord, how much fun you must have, dreaming up blessings to rain down on your children. When I plan the ultimate surprise for my kids, it exhibits just a fraction of the passion with which you imagine the ways you'll surprise and delight me. I remember today that every good thing is from you. Unlike even the most loving and devoted of earthly parents, your affection for me is not subject to my behavior toward you. Even as I selfishly ignore your displays—a brightly blooming azalea, an unexpected check in the mail, a break in the clouds—you continue to fix your thoughts on me. How gratuitous you are, Father, and how very blessed am I!

What good gifts are you expecting today?

Speak of Your Love

If you confess with your mouth the Lord Jesus and believe in your heart that God has raised Him from the dead, you will be saved. For with the heart one believes unto righteousness, and with the mouth confession is made unto salvation.

ROMANS 10: 9–10 NKJV

God, I confess I don't always like to confess. Sometimes, to speak my sin is more than I can bear. What a blessing it is to know that just to confess that Jesus died for me—just to believe in my heart you raised him up—is enough to set me right with you. You make it so easy, Father! To believe and to speak of the incomprehensible love you showed for me by sending your Son to suffer on behalf of all my sins—confessed and unconfessed, past and future—is all you ask. Thank you for your love. I love you too.

Is your heart open to confess Jesus today?

Gentleness That Defies

Remind the people to be subject to rulers and authorities,
to be obedient, to be ready to do whatever is good,
to slander no one, to be peaceable and considerate,
and always to be gentle toward everyone.

TITUS 3:1–2 NIV

Gentle Father, your patience and tenderness are so much more than I deserve. I know you wish me to behave with gentleness toward my children as you have shown to me. I want that too, and when everything is going well, my responses are often tender and understanding. When the pressure is on, though, I can be short-tempered, impatient, and harsh. Show me this tendency as soon as it awakens, Lord, so I can call upon your gentle Spirit to respond on my behalf. Fill me with a gentleness that defies my circumstances, so I can reflect your loving attitude no matter what comes my way.

How did you experience God's gentleness today?

February

Look to the LORD and his
strength; seek his face always.

1 CHRONICLES 16:11 NIV

The First Stone

When they persisted in asking Him, He straightened up,
and said to them, "He who is without sin among you,
let him be the first to throw a stone at her."
JOHN 8:7 NASB

Jesus, only you were without sin, and only you never held anyone's sins against them. I, on the other hand, have a list of ways my family could improve, and I have plenty of thoughts about even strangers I meet and people in the media. Lord, why is it so easy to see the sins of others, and why am I so eager to point them out? Have I never ignored my child, spent money I didn't have, or envied a neighbor's shiny new car? Yet even now, you do not hold this against me. You wait with love as I set down my rock, pick up my cross, and continue on my way. What a gracious, gracious God you are.

What stones do you need to put down?

All I Need

My God will supply every need of yours
according to his riches in glory in Christ Jesus.
PHILIPPIANS 4:19 ESV

Lord, how is it you always know what I need? And how do you never tire of providing for me? Even if a material need goes unmet, you love me so tenderly and specifically, I can count on you for the peace and joy I need to sustain me. In fact, some of the most joyful people I've ever seen are those with little more than your love to sustain them. What trust this inspires in my heart, and what gratitude! And then, what humility; I know I don't deserve it, but that never stops you. Your provision is as endless as your love. Give me a heart as grateful as this knowledge deserves.

Do you trust God to supply all your needs?

Simple Pleasures

The LORD protects the simple;
when I was brought low, he saved me.
PSALM 116:6 NRSV

Father, as brilliant as vast and holy as you are, you still make it simple for me to please you. In fact, the simpler I live, the easier it is to honor you with my life. The more I amass—things, responsibilities, distractions—the easier it is to lose sight of the simple pleasure of being your child and raising my own. Don't let me miss the sweetness of my baby's giggle or the beauty of my teenager's smile because of busyness. Don't let the smell of freshly baked bread go unappreciated because I'm in a hurry. Urge me to slow down, take notice, and enjoy these simple pleasures with you. It is here you protect my heart, and here I am most pleasing to you.

How do you enjoy the simple things in life?

Power Supply

He gives power to the faint,
and strengthens the powerless.
ISAIAH 40:29 NRSV

God with the strength that moves mountains, I could use a hand today. Managing this household is a huge task, feeling bigger on some days than others. I know you know how heavy this load is, and you wouldn't ask me to carry it without a reason, but I really don't think I can do it without you anymore. Is that why you gave it to me? So I'd remember I don't have to do it alone—to do anything alone? You are my power supply, Lord. How silly I must look to you, trying to chug along my own steam when you have all I need and more, just waiting to be given. I'm ready to receive it, Father, and more grateful than I can express.

How do you feel God strengthening you today?

No Small Miracle

You are the God who performs miracles;
you display your power among the peoples.
PSALM 77:14 NIV

God of miracles, your work is on display for all who choose to see. Every day the blind still see, the lame still walk, and the hardest of hearts are turned to you. Just the fact I am here with my family is no small miracle. How many times have you plucked us from danger or even death that I know nothing about? Nothing is too hard for you. Nothing asked from a heart that's tuned to yours is too much to ask. How can this be? You amaze me. And most amazing of all, you love to do it! You want me to ask for hard things—impossible things—so here I go: go ahead, Lord. Amaze me again.

Is your heart open to expecting a miracle?

Inspired to Please

"Be careful! When you do good things, don't do them in front of people to be seen by them. If you do that, you will have no reward from your Father in heaven."

MATTHEW 6:1 NCV

Lord, anything I achieve is because of your favor, and yours is the only recognition I need. Yet I confess I want the approval of others as well. I want people to notice how well I've dressed the kids, or how nicely they share with others. It feels good to be recognized, especially for doing what I love. Only you know my heart, Father. Even more so than I, you know whether I am sharing my pictures on social media to inspire others to action...or to get admiration. One ambition is pleasing to you, and the other is not. Search my heart, Lord, and inspire me to please you!

Who are you trying to please today?

Confidence

Do not throw away your confidence, which has a great reward.
HEBREWS 10:35 NCV

Lord Jesus, there are so many things to admire about you, so many things to learn from your perfect example. Today I am meditating on your confidence. That very first miracle, when the water became the finest wine, did you doubt—even for a second—that it would? Even once as you healed someone, did you wonder, what if it doesn't work this time? Of course you didn't; you had the confidence of the Father, the same assurance available to me. Help me remember, Lord, that I can approach the throne with authority. You gave me that right when I confessed my belief in you. You will help me do all that needs to be done today. Don't let me throw away my confidence on something as worthless as doubt.

How do you place your confidence in your heavenly Father?

You Remain Faithful

If we are faithless, he remains faithful—
for he cannot deny himself.
2 TIMOTHY 2:13 ESV

Faithful God. I just want to stop for a moment and consider what that means—faithful God. You are the perfect one, the one who deserves all my devotion, yet you are the one who remains committed to me, no matter how many times I let you down. There is no end to your awesomeness, Lord, and daily I benefit. Allow the knowledge of your unwavering faithfulness to birth in me a fresh level of devotion to you. Allow my growing faithfulness to you to spill over into my relationships with my children so that I, like you, will be known for my steadfastness. You can only be what you are, which is perfect, and I can only be what I am, which is grateful and humbled.

How do you see God's faithfulness in your life today?

Everything Changes

Be diligent in these matters; give yourself wholly to them,
so that everyone may see your progress.
1 TIMOTHY 4:15 NIV

Unchanging Lord, how intriguing that you created a world where nothing stays the same. Only you are perfect, so everything else must change. The color of the sky changes minute to minute, and even the hardest of rocks wear down with time. Perhaps most striking of all, I am never the same person upon rising as I was the day before. Though as granite, wear away at my heart, hardened by time and experience, until it is as soft and warm as yours. Let all my growth and change be toward becoming more like you, Father, and let my children recognize and be drawn to you in me.

How are you changing to become more like Jesus?

Light, Love, and Truth

Peter and the apostles replied,
"We must obey God rather than any human."
ACTS 5:29 NLT

Sovereign God, this is your world. I am your child.
An outsider wouldn't know it most days, as I'm often
calling my own shots and making my own rules,
but I do believe it. I'm even glad of it, which is also
seldom obvious. Please forgive my disobedience!
Obeying your call means walking in light, living in
love, speaking truth. Why would I want to resist?
Holy Spirit, I need your help! Remind me how warm
the light is, how sweet the love, how priceless the
truth. I must obey you as I ask my children to obey
me. Not because you demand it, but because it gives
life meaning.

Is your meaning in life based on God's truth?

The Mirror

If anyone is in Christ, there is a new creation: everything old
has passed away; see, everything has become new!
2 CORINTHIANS 5:17 NRSV

Lord, you make all things new. The moment I chose
to love you, you began a transforming work in me.
You washed me clean. Years of sin, guilt, regret, and
grime—gone! It's more than I can grasp, this new
self. As incredible as it is, I believe I am forgiven. But
new? Changed? I don't know. Help me understand
that the old self, the one that needed defenses,
regrets, grudges, and contention, is truly gone. Bring
me to your mirror, Father, and linger with me until I
comprehend that this loving, joyful, gracious, peaceful
person is me! I have become new.

How do you see yourself in God's mirror?

Not Good

I know what it is to be in need, and I know what it is
to have plenty. I have learned the secret of being content
in any and every situation, whether well fed or hungry,
whether living in plenty or in want.

PHILIPPIANS 4:12 NIV

Lord, you are good! You are good when things are good, and you are good when they are not. To fix my attention on you ensures I have contentment. This is easy to see on the great days: things go well, so I feel blessed. On the bad days, I have to look deeper— maybe deeper than I can look on my own. In the midst of disconcerting news or disappointing results, remind me to call on your Holy Spirit for strength! Let me see that even on my worst day, you are there to bless me and my family with a surge of contentment or a glimpse of joy. When things are not good, let me know your goodness and I will be blessed.

How can you trust God for contentment in every situation?

Let You In

Search me, O God, and know my heart;
test me and know my anxious thoughts.
PSALM 139:23 NLT

God who sees even what I imagine, who hears what I think but do not say, how deeply you must love me to forgive even my ugliest thoughts. At times I want to hide the worst of it from you: the jealousy, anger, and fear, but then I am overwhelmed by the depth of your love and all I want is to let you in further. What else am I hiding, Father? Is there anything tucked away in my heart that keeps me from you? I think of my child trying to hide something from me when I know full well it is there. Help me to show you everything, so you can forgive it all, change it all, and replace it all with love.

How far are you willing to let God search your heart?

You Are Love

He who does not love does not know God, for God is love.
1 JOHN 4:8 NKJV

God, you are love. You are selfless, forgiving, generous, patient, kind, and so much more. I want to know it all—the much and the more. I'm so grateful for earthly love, for the glimpses it offers me of who you are. Every hug or butterfly kiss from my kids is an example of your tenderness, every sacrifice a symbol of your devotion. As I experience love, I experience you—oh, how I thank you! Thank you for giving yourself to me in millions of ways over thousands of days. Nothing compares to you.

How have you seen God's love for you and your children today?

One Heart

"I will give them one heart, and put a new spirit within them. And I will take the heart of stone out of their flesh and give them a heart of flesh."

EZEKIEL 11:19 NASB

Lord, I love imagining a world where every heart is yours. I picture an end to hunger, to war, and to oppression. None of those things would exist if we all had hearts that beat for you. How could anyone be hungry when none of us could bear it? Who would there be to fight against, if we were of one heart? Remove our cold hearts; replace them with pieces of yours. What could be more beautiful than to see you reflected in every face, and to know everyone I meet is truly my brother or sister? Is this heaven I imagine? If so, then heaven, come!

Is your heart one with God's heart?

Every Opportunity

Let us not grow weary while doing good,
for in due season we shall reap if we do not lose heart.
GALATIANS 6:9 NKJV

Lord, how do you not need rest? Just thinking about your constant attention to my needs makes me tired, and I am just one of your beloved children. I wonder what it would be like to have the means, energy, and enthusiasm to seize every opportunity to do good. Help me, Holy Spirit. Show me where I can be of use and fill me with an energy that doesn't fade—even when met with aching muscles, competing desires, or ungrateful recipients. I know you are there, in the midst of the good, and I don't want to miss an opportunity to meet with you.

How do you keep from growing weary in doing good?

Illusion of Control

Give yourselves completely to God. Stand against the devil,
and the devil will run from you.
JAMES 4:7 NASB

Perfect Lord, why is it so hard to surrender to you?
I'm afraid of not having control, but the truth is, I
don't have it anyway. I can hardly control myself,
let alone the children in my care. I am controlled by
the idea that I need to make my own decisions, fight
my own battles. I know it's the enemy who tries to
convince me to hold myself back, and I know it's
because he cannot stand against you. If I am all
yours, he has no choice but to leave. Help me, Holy
Spirit. Pry open my fingers when I cling to the illusion
of control. Stretch open my hands and help me lift
them heavenward. I hand over my life to you; all my
decisions and battles are yours—I am free.

**How have you given yourself completely to God so
that you are free?**

Anger Rising

"In your anger do not sin": Do not let
the sun go down while you are still angry.
EPHESIANS 4:26 NIV

Lord, your Word tells me you are slow to anger.
I cannot always say the same of myself. Some
days, it takes little more than a child's complaint
or a missed school bus to provoke me. The whole
trajectory of my day hinges on whether my next
move is toward sin or toward you. I confess there
are plenty of days where I move the wrong way. A
harsh word or hasty action follows, and to make
matters worse, I sometimes hang onto my anger
for the rest of the day—as if it were a lifeline. This
further separates me from you, which is the last thing
I want. When I feel anger rising, Lord, let your love
and forgiveness rise faster.

What made you angry today? Can you let it go?

Calm, Measured Steps

We also pray that you will be strengthened
with all his glorious power so you will have
all the endurance and patience you need.
COLOSSIANS 1:11 NLT

Father, your patience amazes me again and again,
and I know the qualities you show most often are the
ones you'd most like to see in me. When I'm in the
middle of a trial (and when am I not?), it pleases you
to see me respond with patience. It proves I trust you,
proves I believe you, proves I love you. Forgive me
for how often I struggle against my circumstances.
Like a marathon runner at mile fourteen who begins
to run in place, or even backward, how silly I must
seem to you. Calm, measured, forward steps are what
carry me toward you. Grant me endurance, Lord, as I
continue on my way.

**How can you trust God's power for endurance and
patience?**

Pursued by Goodness

Surely goodness and mercy shall follow me
All the days of my life;
And I will dwell in the house of the LORD
Forever.
PSALM 23:6 NKJV

Lord, thank you for your goodness and for the assurance in your Word that with you as my shepherd, that goodness follows me wherever I go. What a beautiful image, being pursued by goodness! I can't help but consider how often I must appear to be trying to outrun it as I chase after the things in front of me each day and try to corral those precious children who seem to run in different directions at the same time. My prayer today is that I would slow down enough to be overrun by you— that I would turn around, arms open, and fling myself wholeheartedly into your goodness.

How can you sense God's presence following you?

Separated from Guilt

Since we have been justified by faith, we have peace
with God through our Lord Jesus Christ.
ROMANS 5:1 ESV

God of peace, how do I accept what I do not deserve? Though I am guilty of many things, you release me from all of it. You send my shame to the bottom of the ocean. You separate me from my guilt as the east is from the west. The unfairness of it goes against my human reasoning, so I resist this gift, sometimes even diving down to reclaim it. If I don't feel guilty, won't that mean I am not sorry? I wonder. No, you answer, it will mean you have replaced your sorrow with my peace. Thank you, Father. Your gifts are so very, very good. Help me to offer the same forgiveness and kindness to my children when they are disobedient, rude, or unruly. Let me show them they don't need to wallow in guilt as I am apt to do.

Do you need God's peace today?

Far Away

In God, whose word I praise,
In God I have put my trust;
I shall not be afraid.
What can mere man do to me?
PSALM 56:4 NASB

Father, you are so faithful. As I pause and consider the times you've removed an obstacle from my path, made a way where there was none, I know you can do anything. These young ones that I love so dearly need your help, Lord. We might not be able to see the way through, but I know you do. Our enemy wants us focused on the obstacle, so we forget we have you, our great intercessor. He wants us trusting our own efforts or giving up entirely. Help us to trust you, Father, as we place this matter before you. Lift our eyes off the problem and onto you, then lift the problem and take it far away.

What problem needs to be taken far away from you today?

Restraint

"Put your sword back in its place," Jesus said to him,
"for all who draw the sword will die by the sword.
Do you think I cannot call on my Father, and he will at once put
at my disposal more than twelve legions of angels."
MATTHEW 26:52–53 NIV

Jesus, you were fully human while you were here, so I can imagine how tempting it must have been to silence your detractors, to cure every ill. When I consider your restraint, I realize I need to call on your Spirit for my own control. I have a hard time resisting an argument, even with my children whom I love so dearly, but I know peace is the path you'd have me walk. Comfort and relaxation call my name, though I know you have still more for me to do. I need your self-control, Holy Spirit. Fill me with restraint and a longing for the peace it brings.

Where do you need God's restraint today?

Move Me

> When He saw the multitudes, He was moved
> with compassion for them, because they were weary
> and scattered, like sheep having no shepherd.
> MATTHEW 9:36 NKJV

Merciful Lord, you see our desperation and you cannot stay where you are. You long to intercede. As soon as we ask, you respond. Compassion moves you. How often do I say I am moved, yet I remain exactly where I am? When will I learn that feeling sorry about suffering is not equal to moving to end it? Move me, God! Show me something that breaks your heart, and let it break mine. Let the pain I feel for my children pluck me from my comfort and place me right in the middle of their suffering, ready, willing, and even desperate to act.

Where do you want God to move your heart?

Tune Me

I want you to understand what really matters, so that you may
live pure and blameless lives until the day of Christ's return.
PHILIPPIANS 1:9–10 NLT

God, you are so wise! You always know what is
right, and I need some of that wisdom for myself.
When I rely on my own judgment, as I too often do,
it's easy to get confused. Remind me what really
matters, Lord, as I try to discern between your voice
and all the others. Tune me, like a radio frequency, to
your will today, God. Let the voice of the enemy be
nothing but static—or a song so out of tune I can't
bear to listen. Your will is the sweetest sound I know,
and to know it is all I ask.

Are you tuned to God's frequency?

Sit and Wait

Wait for the LORD;
be strong, and let your heart take courage;
wait for the LORD!
PSALM 27:14 NRSV

God, you have perfect timing. I'm not great at remembering this. I think my answers should come now; the solutions I seek be only days away. My days move forward all too quickly and I get anxious thinking you have not heard me. You see the whole picture, though, and sometimes I'm just going to have to wait for you. For those times, Father, I call on your strength. Give me the courage to sit here and wait. I can hear the thunder. My instincts are telling me to run, though I know you can change the path of the storm. Send your Spirit to quiet my heart while I wait.

Do you struggle with waiting for the Lord?

Releasing Kindness

"Love your enemies, and do good, and lend,
expecting nothing in return, and your reward will be great,
and you will be sons of the Most High, for he
is kind to the ungrateful and the evil."

LUKE 6:35 ESV

Father, your incredible kindness illustrates the value you place on it. It pleases you to show kindness to me, and likewise when I am kind to others. I do love to please you, and what does it cost me to smile, to compliment my child, to wrap them in my arms? Would you move through a room and not acknowledge me? Why, then, do I keep my head down? Help me release your kindness into this house, God. Lift my eyes and open my mouth and let your beauty spill forth.

Who can you release kindness to today?

Awe Inspired

"His mercy extends to those who fear him,
from generation to generation."
LUKE 1:50 NIV

Lord, nothing deserves more respect than you.
We know to respect the power of the ocean or the
storm, yet we fail to honor the one who made it, who
tells it how far to go. We take advantage of your love
for us, and it manifests as disrespect. The mercy
you show us, even then, calls for even more respect.
Thank you, God, for the awe you inspire. Thank you
for your limitless love and forgiveness. You deserve
all my respect, all my love, all my praise. I offer them
to you now and always in the name of Jesus.

Are you in awe of the Lord?

Replacing Worry

Do not worry about anything, but pray and ask God for
everything you need, always giving thanks. And God's peace,
which is so great we cannot understand it, will keep your
hearts and minds in Christ Jesus.

PHILIPPIANS 4:6–7 NCV

Gracious God, because of you, I don't need to hold
onto worry. Each time anxiety rises in me, I can come
to you with my problem, laying my burden at your
feet. You promise help. Even if you don't change my
circumstances, you give me your peace, so I can endure
the waiting. I can't imagine how it's possible. How, when
someone I love is in danger, am I able to smile? How,
when the bank balance is too small, am I able to laugh?
It shouldn't be so, yet you prove it each time I trust you.
Fill me now, Lord, with your peace. Replace my worry
with the assurance of your provision.

**What are you worrying about? Can you replace it with
God's peace?**

March

We are confident that he
hears us whenever
we ask for anything
that pleases him.

1 John 5:14 nlt

Change Is Good

Anyone who belongs to Christ has become a new person.
The old life is gone; a new life has begun!
2 CORINTHIANS 5:17 NLT

Lord, you are constant. Your love, once accepted, cannot be returned. You ended my old life, renewed my old self. I am forever changed by your unchanging love. Most days, this brings me such joy! It is so much better to spend my days with you than in my old, empty pursuits. But there are other days. like a new pair of jeans, sometimes this new life feels a little scratchy, a little stiff. Will you help me through it, Father? Remind me that change is good, even when I'm doubting it? Stay with me in this new place until it fits like a second skin?

Have you found a new place in Christ? Are you comfortable with it yet?

Buckling Knees

Fear not, for I am with you;
be not dismayed, for I am your God;
I will strengthen you, I will help you,
I will uphold you with my righteous right hand.
ISAIAH 41:10 ESV

God who supplies all courage, I feel like I keep coming back to this well again and again. Did you design me this way, so I'd return to you each time I needed filling up? How grateful I am for your endless supply, and how lost I'd be without it. Life is scary, Father. Of course, you know that. That's why you stick so close, ready to hold me up each time my knees buckle. Like a child inspecting beneath the bed, bolstered by the courage of Daddy holding the flashlight, I am encouraged by your presence. I can face this; I have nothing to fear.

Do you need filling up? Do you know that God is there for you?

Faith Spilling Over

> "All things you ask in prayer, believing, you will receive."
> MATTHEW 21:22 NASB

All-powerful God, nothing is beyond your ability, no matter how audacious. And no matter how simple, no sincere prayer is unworthy of your consideration. You delight in answering our faithful prayers. You wait, eagerly and filled with joy, as my children and I ask you for help. A heart turned entirely to you will not ask for anything you don't want it to have. A heart filled to overflowing with faith will not doubt your response. It is these things I ask for, for myself and my children: a heart that is yours, faith spilling over, anticipating your answer.

Do you believe you can be spilling over with faith?

A Place for Me

"There are many rooms in my Father's house;
I would not tell you this if it were not true.
I am going there to prepare a place for you."
JOHN 14:2 NCV

God in heaven, how often I imagine you there, and I try to imagine my life there with you. I think of moving to a new house as a child. The first thing I want to see, before the kitchen or the big back yard, is my room. What's it like? Did you bring my pillow, my stuffed animals, my pictures for the wall? Is it true that already, Jesus is preparing a place for me? I can scarcely take it in, a room in your house made just for me—filled with things that show you know me, that you've always known me. Thank you for your abiding love, Father. I can't wait to come home.

Can you imagine what kind of house God is preparing for you in heaven?

For My Mistakes

Though he fall, he shall not be cast headlong,
for the LORD upholds his hand.
PSALM 37:24 ESV

Forgiving Lord, how do you never tire of forgiving my mistakes? In the morning, I promise you a day dedicated to your purpose and fixed on your love, and by noon I am up to my neck in endless mistakes and worthless distractions. I've blown it. Again. And here you are, arms open, proud of me for acknowledging it. How? May I never stop being awed by this. Forgive me, Lord. I'm standing right on the edge, and the only thing keeping me from tripping into emptiness is you. On my knees, I pledge to try harder. And when I fall, I'll thank you for raising me back up once again.

Did you fall today? Do you know that the Lord will pick you back up?

Greater Meaning

"If a man has a hundred sheep but one of the sheep gets lost,
he will leave the other ninety-nine on the hill
and go to look for the lost sheep."
MATTHEW 18:12 NCV

God of the universe, how is it that I matter to you? I think of my mark here—how small and insignificant by human standards—and it just astonishes me that you count me so precious. The significance you give me by caring so deeply inspires me to live a life of greater meaning. Help me be more worthy of your intimate involvement, Lord! Not because you require it, but because your great love is deserving of my best effort. You'd set down your heavy load to give me a hand. You'd leave your flock on the hill, unattended, to search for me. Oh, that I would be worthy of such devotion.

Do you feel like a lost sheep? Do you know that God is looking for you?

Child of the King

Your wife will be like a fruitful grapevine,
flourishing within your home.
Your children will be like vigorous young olive trees
as they sit around your table.

PSALM 128:3 NLT

Father, what a privilege it is to be your child. To call Jesus both Savior and our brother is a gift too precious to comprehend. Thank you for making me such a treasured member of your family! As my thoughts turn to my earthly family, I ask you to bless us. You know the relationships that need healing, the hearts that need protection, and the lives that need restoration. Help us to love each other with gratitude and respect, to honor one another's position as sons and daughters of the Most High King. Heal, protect, and restore us, Lord, in Jesus' name.

Who in your family needs a healing touch from God?

My Help

I lift up my eyes to the hills—
from where will my help come?
My help comes from the LORD,
who made heaven and earth.
PSALM 121:1–2 NRSV

Lord, I need your help. It's true every day, but I'm especially aware today. Responsibilities and burdens weigh me down; I can no longer carry this load. As I crumple under the weight, I lift my eyes. And there you are. Ever-present Lord, you wait for me, always, to look up. Your strong, loving arms are more than capable of this load, and your heart is more than ready to comfort mine. As it all becomes too much, how wonderful to remember that nothing is too much for you. Your help gives me hope, Father. Thank you.

Where do you need God's help today?

Drawing Me Back

May the Lord of peace himself give you peace at all times
in every way. The Lord be with you all.
2 THESSALONIANS 3:16 NIV

God of Peace, thank you for being the source of this most precious and mysterious gift. Your joy makes me happy in every circumstance. And so, too, your peace renders me calm despite even a raging storm of difficulty. I confess I don't always avail myself of these blessings. Allowing stress to take hold, I sometimes leave the calm center and rush off into the driving wind. Even when anxiety would seem to have a death grip on me, your peace draws me back to you. A Scripture comes to mind, or a tune runs through my head, and suddenly, the storm is forgotten. All is calm; all is bright. Peace is here.

Do you know the Lord is with you to give you peace at all times?

Though I Fail

My flesh and my heart may fail,
but God is the strength of my heart
and my portion forever.
PSALM 73:26 NIV

God, you are perfect. It's hard to imagine; even the most exquisite rose has a tiny flaw somewhere, but you have none. You never fail. I wake with such good intentions, Father, but then I get distracted, busy, and overwhelmed with the needs of others. I want to honor you with every minute of my life, but inevitably, I fail. Then I remember Jesus, and I understand how amazing a gift you gave me through him. You knew how weak I would be—how weak all your children are—and you sent him, a perfect sacrifice, to pay for our failures. Though I keep failing, your love never does.

Do you know that God is the strength of your heart, and he is there when you fail?

Too Much to Hold

"Give, and you will receive. You will be given much.
Pressed down, shaken together, and running over,
it will spill into your lap. The way you give to others is
the way God will give to you."

LUKE 6:38 NCV

You are so generous, Lord! Especially when I give generously, your blessings pour back to me. Not only does your joy fill my heart, but you always replace what I give away. Though I know this to be true, I confess I don't always want to give. Don't let those selfish impulses win, Lord! Remind me what else is mine—your joyful presence—and that no thing, or any amount of money, is more valuable to me than that. Inspire me to care more for the comfort of my family and others, God. Move me to share all that's mine. It is more than I can hold anyway.

What can you let go of so God can give you more?

Laying Down Weapons

"The LORD will fight for you, and you shall hold your peace."
EXODUS 14:14 NKJV

Powerful God, what fight is too great for you? Nothing can defeat you: no scheme, no weapon—nothing. Though I know of your great power, I often try to fight my own battles. Sometimes I still scrape by, but how much greater would my victory be if I called upon you? And what of the many times I lie defeated? So unnecessary when I have the God of Angel Armies on my side. I don't want to play general today, God. You know my battle plan, and you know of the enemy's strategy to defeat me. I'm laying down my weapons, taking shelter in your peace, and letting you take over.

Can you trust the Lord to fight your battles today?

The Sweetest Fruit

The fruit of the Spirit is love, joy, peace, forbearance,
kindness, goodness, faithfulness, gentleness and self-control.
Against such things there is no law.
GALATIANS 5:22–23 NIV

Holy Spirit, I want all of you! You are my helper,
my best friend, and the bearer of not just gifts, but
also the sweetest fruit I've ever tasted. You make me
loving, joyful, and peaceful. You give me patience and
selflessness where it is typically lacking. With you I
am kinder and better, gentler and more faithful. When
I notice those qualities slipping away or absent, I
know I need to return to you. Impatience, selfishness,
and frustration are signs I've lost sight of you or
turned my back. Don't let me, please! Help me
remember how lovely it is to live and walk with you,
how much better it is for my children when I am full
of your fruit.

Are you experiencing the fruit of the Spirit?

Break My Heart

He was amazed to see that no one intervened to help
the oppressed. So he himself stepped in to save them
with his strong arm, and his justice sustained him.
ISAIAH 59:16 NLT

Lord, so overflowing with love, how your heart
must break for the suffering of your children! I know
you don't need my help, but I believe it brings you
happiness when we care for each other. It's easy to
get caught up in my own struggles, but I know they
are nothing compared to what some of your precious
children are enduring this very day. Bring me a need
to pray for, God. Break my heart. Give me the gift of
needing to pray, and of knowing just what to say.
Let your goodness fill my heart and give me strength
to fight for those who can't.

Is there someone you can pray for that God has put on
your heart?

Your Motives

Am I now seeking the approval of man, or of God?
Or am I trying to please man? If I were still trying
to please man, I would not be a servant of Christ.
GALATIANS 1:10 ESV

Lord, your motives are always the same. You want to spread your love and to draw all your children to you. I wish I could say the same. A desire for approval and recognition, my own happiness, and even unkindness are sometimes the reasons for the things I do. How I wish it weren't so! Lord, will you do a work in my heart, give me your motives. I hate the ugly, selfish reasons for some of the things I do, and I long for the simple joy of living my life entirely to please you—to gain your approval. Give me a heart that lives only to spread your love, Father.

Are you seeking man's approval or God's?

Live on Purpose

The LORD has made everything for its purpose,
even the wicked for the day of trouble.
PROVERBS 16:4 ESV

Lord, I love how deliberate and intentional you are! In a world that can seem so random, chaotic, and even frightening, it's such a comfort to know you have a purpose for everyone, and that you can bring good out of even the worst situation. I know I often miss the mark when it comes to doing things on purpose. I react to life as it happens, instead of considering what you would have me do. But you give meaning even to those poor choices. God, I intend to live a meaningful life. With your help, I know I can. Please help me realize and embrace the purpose you've set for me and my family. For my day and for my life, let me live on purpose.

Are you living God's purpose for your life?

Before I Speak

To watch over mouth and tongue
is to keep out of trouble.
PROVERBS 21:23 NRSV

God, I seldom need your forgiveness more than for the words I say. How often my tongue gets me into trouble. Your words always give life. Mine are not always so generous. As soon as I've said something unkind, I know it. I long to take it back, but once it's out there, I can only apologize. Please forgive me. Will you help me with this, Lord? Lock my lips and help me think before I speak, especially when I'm agitated. Before I say a word, help me ask myself, is this necessary, true, and kind? Will this build up or tear down? Only then, let me speak. Help me to encourage my children with all that comes out of my mouth. I want them to know your love for them as I know your love for me.

Do you think before you speak? Are you saying something Jesus would say?

What Is True

I could have no greater joy than to hear
that my children are following the truth.
3 JOHN 1:4 NLT

God, you are truth. Everything you've said or done is honest, right, and good. How very untrue this is of me. I don't even know why I lie. I tell myself it doesn't matter, but that isn't true either. Even to myself, I am dishonest, saying I'll do something later; insisting something didn't hurt me; pretending I don't know I'm about to sin. Lord, because you are truth, I want to value it as I value you. Point out the lies I tell myself, replacing them with truth. Stop me before a dishonest word leaves my mouth, giving me the most loving way to say instead what is true. Starting at this very moment, let me love the truth.

Are you speaking the truth?

Light of Approval

Indeed, by faith our ancestors received approval.
HEBREWS 11:2 NRSV

Lord, I know I'm already accepted by you, and I am grateful beyond words. I don't need to do anything more than accept what's been done for me on the cross, but I still long to please you. Your acceptance guarantees my future, but your approval is what makes my days. Each time I act in a way you would not approve of, I feel your disappointment alongside my own. Show me ways, God, to delight you. Help me believe the work has already been done, but encourage me to work anyway, just to make you happy. Like my child basking in the glow of my admiration, I want to live in the light of your approval and conduct myself in a way that makes you proud.

Do you know that you are accepted by God?

Where Contentment Lives

I am not saying this because I am in need, for I have learned to
be content whatever the circumstances.
PHILIPPIANS 4:11 NIV

God of contentment, you bring me such peace.
I forget this sometimes when my situation becomes
difficult; I take my eyes off you, where perfect peace
resides, and I focus all my attention on the problem.
This brings the opposite of contentment and is not
at all how I wish to live. Lift my chin, Father, when I
drop my eyes from yours. Remind me that your arms
are the safest place, the best place, the only place
contentment lives. Show me the situation for what
it is—a distraction—then allow me to rest in the
knowledge that all will be well. Because of you,
I know this is true.

**Are you learning to be content whatever the
circumstances?**

No Need to Fear

I asked the LORD for help, and he answered me.
He saved me from all that I feared.
PSALM 34:4 NCV

Faithful God, with you I have no need of fear. This doesn't stop me, of course. I become afraid all the time. Fear feels like a living thing. Like it's come in and taken hold of my thoughts, lying to me and trying to convince me I can't rely on you to save me and my family. Sometimes I listen to the lie, and I begin to doubt you. But here you are, again, always reassuring me. I need only speak your name, ask for your help, and fear retreats like a frightened animal. I speak it again, and fear begins to appear silly. Once more, and fear is gone. Thank you, Lord, for the saving power of your name.

What fear can the Lord save you from today?

Your Will Be Done

"Your kingdom come.
Your will be done,
On earth as it is in heaven."
MATTHEW 6:10 NASB

God, your will be done. How many times have I said this? Have I considered, really, what I am praying for? I suspect I don't really want it, deep down. My will be done sounds pretty good, to be honest. I ask for what I want, then add, almost as an afterthought, but only if you will it, Father. All the while, my heart silently begs that you do. Lord, I want to pray it and mean it! I want a heart that is so in tune with yours, I can't even begin to want something out of our will. Confidently, expectantly, I want to say, your will be done, because I know with all I am that this will bring me joy.

Can you confidently ask God for his will to be done?

Not Helpless

When the righteous cry for help, the LORD hears
and delivers them out of all their troubles.
PSALM 34:17 ESV

Gracious Lord, with you there is no such condition
as helpless. It may take us a while to remember
this at times; we'll work until we've exhausted all
our ideas and gone through every human channel.
Desolation knocks on the door, but because of you,
we don't have to answer. God, how can I thank you
for giving me and my children a way through, always,
no matter how bleak things may look? We can
always call on you and you will always answer. Help
me believe this, act on this, and know that whatever
answer you give, it is for my good.

What trouble has the Lord delivered you from lately?

With Your Joy

Rejoice in the Lord always; again I will say, rejoice!
PHILIPPIANS 4:4 NASB

Lord, thank you for joy. What a wonderful gift, to be truly glad no matter how things look or what situation I am in! I don't always acknowledge it. In fact, some days I stubbornly choose not to see it. The situation is hard, and I want to wallow. Like any good friend, you allow it—for a time. Quietly, you and your joy sit and wait for me, knowing I can't resist. Truly, I just can't get over it. In the middle of my deepest sorrow, you are there with your joy. Right at the center of a frustrating, stubborn problem, the joy of the Lord pops in with an explicable lightness and carries me home.

How can you embrace the Lord's joy today?

Surrendered Mind

To set the mind on the flesh is death,
but to set the mind on the Spirit is life and peace.
ROMANS 8:6 NRSV

Brilliant, thoughtful Lord, could I handle your thoughts, even for an instant? My own mind is so full, and so much of it does me no good. Even when I am worshiping you, I allow distractions in. Even as I enjoy the people I love, my mind wanders to places I don't even want to go. Holy Spirit, take over! Capture my thoughts, especially when they wander, and return them continually to the love, the beauty, the endless perfection of our God. I surrender my mind to your will. Please, have your way.

How have you surrendered your mind to God?

Repentance Matters

"Repent of your sins and turn to God,
for the Kingdom of Heaven is near."
MATTHEW 3:2 NLT

Lord, you are so forgiving. Even if I never ask
for it, you offer your forgiveness for every wrong:
past, present, and future. Still, you want me to ask.
Repentance matters to you, so I want it to matter
to me. Show me my sins, so I can hate them as you
do. I want to bring you glory with my life, so send
your Spirit to help me see all the ways I need to be
forgiven. You are right here, Lord, living inside me.
Help me make my heart a worthy home.

Is your heart a worthy home for Jesus?

Cannot Be Tempted

Let no one say when he is tempted,
"I am tempted by God"; for God cannot be tempted
by evil, nor does He Himself tempt anyone.
JAMES 1:13 NKJV

God who cannot be tempted, lend that power to me! I know you allow temptations of all kinds to teach me and strengthen me. Allow me also the ability to resist as you do, immediately and completely, anything that threatens to take me from your will. Thank you for being with me as I face into the things that distract me, things that will bring me only harm. Let me see, even in the moment of greatest weakness, that if it were good, I wouldn't have to hesitate. Help me use this knowledge to run the other way, straight into you.

Do you know that Jesus is waiting for you to run away from evil and run toward him?

Not My Home

Do not conform to the pattern of this world,
but be transformed by the renewing of your mind.
Then you will be able to test and approve what God's will is—
his good, pleasing and perfect will.
ROMANS 12:2 NIV

Perfect Lord, you made this world so lovely, and you have given me so much to appreciate, that sometimes I lose sight of the fact that this is not my home. If the things of this world were what mattered, and if this were all there is, you would be here too. Help me continue to appreciate all that is good here, including my beautiful children and the roof over our heads, but also to resist the lure of thinking that worldly goods are enough. Give me a taste only for what is pleasing to you, Father. Let that be all that matters to me.

Are you living like this world is not your home?

Selfish Ambition

"Whoever exalts himself will be humbled,
and whoever humbles himself will be exalted."
MATTHEW 23:12 ESV

Most High God, from the very beginning, we've wondered what it would be like to sit atop your throne. We see your glory and want to feel it for ourselves. You give us a tiny fraction of your talent, the littlest bit of your brilliance, and we imagine a future filled with praise. I know I'm guilty; a little recognition goes right to my head, and I begin to think I deserve it. I start to crave it. Forgive me for my selfish ambition, Father. When someone shines a spotlight on a talent or quality of mine, let me step to the side and allow your own radiance to take over. Let all my ambition be aimed glorifying you.

Do you know that God wants to exalt you?

April

You will call on me and
come and pray to me,
and I will listen to you.

JEREMIAH 29:12 NIV

Who Can Criticize

Keep a good conscience so that in the thing
in which you are slandered, those who revile
your good behavior in Christ will be put to shame.
1 PETER 3:16 NASB

God, who can know you and criticize you? You are perfect, and all your ways are wonderful. Those who don't know you may think they have something to say, and they may criticize me for my devotion to you. Let them talk. When I consider my life before you, or imagine my life without you, all I see is emptiness. People who resent my hope, envy my peace, or misunderstand your goodness can say what they want. With your help, I'll live a life that gives them nothing new to add to their complaint. In fact, your light in me may just change their minds. Let it be so, Lord!

Do you realize that God's light in you can change people's minds about you and him?

Prone to Wander

LORD, I know that people's lives are not their own;
it is not for them to direct their steps.

JEREMIAH 10:23 NIV

God, how wonderful it is to follow you! I don't have to know where I'm going or worry about leading my children onto the wrong path. There is such freedom in knowing you know exactly where I need to go, and you will do everything necessary to get me there. Even if I wander—and we both know I will—your brilliant light will show me the way back. Shine brightly, Lord, so brightly I can't possibly miss you. I'm prone to wander and stubborn enough to want to make my own way sometimes. Help me follow willingly, God, so that anyone looking to me for direction will not miss you, either.

How are you following God's footsteps for your life?

You Are Perfect

As for God, His way is perfect;
The word of the LORD is proven;
He is a shield to all who trust in Him.
PSALM 18:30 NKJV

Lord, can I just bathe in your perfection today? I want to take it in, be overwhelmed by all the ways you are perfect, until it is too much for me to contain. It's so much to strive for, the call to be like you, but what a wonderful way to pass the time! I have no request, Lord; I only want to celebrate you. As I reflect on your perfect love, forgiveness, peace, provision, protection, and more, keep bringing to mind even more of the ways you amaze me. Keep showing me new things to strive for, new ways to be grateful, new ways to demonstrate your love and goodness to my children.

Are you ready to bathe in God's perfection and be overwhelmed by his ways?

Source of Hope

I pray that God, the source of hope, will fill you completely with
joy and peace because you trust in him.
Then you will overflow with confident hope through
the power of the Holy Spirit.
ROMANS 15:13 NLT

God, your Word tells me that your joy and peace bring hope, a confident belief in wonderful things I can't yet see. I may need help remembering this from time to time, when worries and problems cloud my vision. I get full of so many things, Lord. Tasks and schedules take up space in my head, crowding out joy and peace—and the hope that accompanies them. When the way seems hopeless, remind me to call on you. You are the source. Empty me of joy stealers and peace killers, then fill me to overflowing with hope.

How are the things of the world crowding out your peace and joy?

Desiring Humility

The reward for humility and fear of the LORD
is riches and honor and life.
PROVERBS 22:4 ESV

Lord, your rewards are so generous, and by
comparison, your demands are small. You desire humility,
and in exchange you promise exaltation. Perhaps
that's what makes it so hard to achieve; we desire the
reward and in the wanting, humility slips through our
fingers. Thank you for reminding me, through your own
perfection, how very small I am, how much growing I
have to do. Help me to be reminded of this as I consider
my own children and how much they have left to grow.
Thank you for daily opportunities to earn your rich
reward as I recognize my own limitations, in parenting
and in life, and learn to rely on your greatness.

**How do your own limitations bring you closer to relying
on God's greatness?**

Cannot Be Lost

Every valley shall be raised up,
every mountain and hill made low;
the rough ground shall become level,
the rugged places a plain.
ISAIAH 40:4 NIV

Father, thank you for being constant. Loss leaves me feeling lost; grief is like a mountain with no discernible path. The way seems so unclear, the terrain unnavigable. I'm afraid if I raise my head, I'll fall right off the edge. But then I remember your promises, and I lift my eyes. You are here, right where you've always been, making a new way for me. Lord, please protect me from the temptation to look down, to focus on how impossible this new climb seems. Smooth out the rough places; I can't do this life without your help. I need wisdom, grace, and strength to raise these children. Step by step, day by day, keep my eyes fixed on what I cannot lose.

Are you looking to Jesus for each step and keeping your focus on him?

Renew My Mind

Let the Spirit renew your thoughts and attitudes.
EPHESIANS 4:23 NLT

Lord, what is more difficult to control than the mind? If I could stop my anxious thoughts, if I could keep selfish ideas from even forming, it would be so much easier to stay in your will! If only I had a mind like Christ, instead of the inconstancy of my own. Holy Spirit, always here and ready to help, I need you to renew my mind. Replace every unworthy thought before I am even aware of it with something beautiful, pure, and true. Instead of fear, let me see an opportunity to trust. Rather than self-interest, show me a chance for self-sacrifice. Instead of my mind, give me the mind of Christ.

How do you let the Spirit renew your thoughts and attitudes?

Made to Be

Since we have gifts that differ according to the grace
given to us, each of us is to exercise them accordingly.
ROMANS 12:6 NASB

Lord, I love how individually you made each of us.
It further illustrates your awesomeness that there are
so many gifts, all present in you, distributed among
even my small family. Thank you for the specific and
unique way you have gifted us, some so attentive to
the passions and talents already present in us, and
others so surprisingly new. We are never so alive as
when using the talents or exercising the passions you
put inside us for your glory. To be who you made us
to be, and to do it for you, is the greatest gift
we know.

How has God made you unique?

Wise Enough

If any of you is lacking in wisdom, ask God, who gives to all generously and ungrudgingly, and it will be given you.
JAMES 1:5 NRSV

Wise and wonderful God, why do I look anywhere else for answers? Who besides you knows me and my children so well, and loves us so completely? Only you know all there is to know, yet I seek solutions in so many places before I come to you. Forgive me, Lord. I have so many questions, and you have all the answers. I seek knowledge, goodness, and truth; you are these things. Make me wise enough to remember this when I'm tempted to look elsewhere. Dear God, grant me wisdom of my own. Most especially, I pray for the wisdom to go first and always to you, wisdom's only true source.

Are you lacking wisdom? Have you asked God for it?

Willing Submission

Obey your leaders and act under their authority. They are watching over you, because they are responsible for your souls. Obey them so that they will do this work with joy, not sadness. It will not help you to make their work hard.

HEBREWS 13:17 NCV

Lord God, you are the true authority, so I should remember—and trust—that anyone with authority over me has it with your approval. We're so very young when we start to struggle against this idea! As soon as my children had a will, they began to exert it and to resist anyone who tried to control any aspect of their lives. Like the toddler who insisted on putting on her own shoes—when to allow Mama would have been so much simpler—I still struggle when I lack control over my situation. Holy Spirit, please subdue me! Show me the gift of willing submission, and the peace that comes by trusting that any authority you have placed over me is for my good.

Do you struggle with submission? Can you trust God through those who are placed over you?

Self-Discipline

Since we are surrounded by so great a cloud of witnesses, let us also lay aside every weight, and sin which clings so closely, and let us run with endurance the race that is set before us.
HEBREWS 12:1 ESV

Lord, your Word tells me you are not the only one watching: all of heaven rejoices when one of your children finds the truth, and the angels hang on our actions, minor and monumental. What a spectacle we must be! This awareness, when I recall it, motivates me to choose well, to work hard, to run long. Thank you for that! And merciful God, forgive me for the times I forget it. Lord, help me to love self-discipline. I want to make all of heaven proud, especially you, and this requires an awareness of you—of all of you—and the incredible legacy I am a part of as one of your family.

Do you realize the incredible legacy you have as part of God's family?

My Real Future

Come now, you who say, "Today or tomorrow we will go to such and such a town and spend a year there, doing business and making money." Yet you do not even know what tomorrow will bring. What is your life? For you are a mist that appears for a little while and then vanishes. Instead you ought to say, "If the LORD wishes, we will live and do this or that."

JAMES 4:13–15 NRSV

Lord, you know my future; you planned it. I have dreams and I make plans, and I know much of my ambition for the future comes from you. Yet I also know I can easily get ahead of myself—assuming I have years or even weeks I may not have. Lord, help me to focus on the immediate future, on what I will do with this next minute, not the next year or next chapter. Remind me to pursue your purpose so that whichever minute marks the end of my earthly future, it has poised me for my real future with you.

How can you be focused on the immediate future and pursue God's purpose for your life?

You Are Present

No one has ever seen God. But if we love each other,
God lives in us, and his love is brought to full expression in us.
1 JOHN 4:12 NLT

Lord, nothing compares to your presence. In the church building, surrounded by beautiful music and other believers there to meet with you, it's tangible. Your joy invades my soul, and I know you are there. Away from the sanctuary, I long for you; I seek your presence everywhere I go. And then your Word reminds me. Because I love, you are present inside me. I need only to love to find you. What a gift! Just to think of my beloved children, and to feel the warmth and peace that accompanies their image, is to experience you. To tell them of my love is to tell of yours. Thank you, Father, for the incomparable gift of your presence in my own heart.

Can you take time today to feel God's presence in your heart?

Still Promised

"For I know the plans I have for you," declares the LORD,
"plans to prosper you and not to harm you,
plans to give you hope and a future."
JEREMIAH 29:11 NIV

Loving Father, from the moment you dreamed me up and began numbering the hairs on my head, you planned the many blessings you'd rain down on my life—including the children you have placed in my care. The plans and dreams of an earthly father are just an inkling, a mere glimpse of the hope and promise you hold in your heart, ready to pour into mine. Help me to trust always that your plans are best, that your hope for my life is greater than I can imagine. Help me face boldly, gladly into your plans. I thank you for all you've done for me, and I marvel at the thought of all you still promise to do. You love me so well, Father!

Do you know that God has plans to give you hope and a future?

No Room for Jealousy

Wrath is fierce and anger is a flood,
But who can stand before jealousy?
PROVERBS 27:4 NASB

Lord, you grant peace and humility, leaving no room for jealousy. When I am close to you, I have all I could possibly want, freeing me to be truly happy for blessings in the lives of others. Why do I allow myself to get far enough from your comforting presence to invite envy into my heart? I can see it brings nothing of beauty into my life. In fact, it brings me low. Father, forgive me for feeling I need or deserve something you haven't chosen to give me. I am ashamed of these thoughts; therefore, I know they are not from you. Draw me back to contentment, where I can stand with you. Let me demonstrate that kind of life to my children, so they are also content in only you.

Are you content with Jesus only?

My Reconciliation

If while we were enemies we were reconciled to God
by the death of his Son, much more, now that we
are reconciled, shall we be saved by his life.
ROMANS 5:10 ESV

Gracious Lord, you forgave me for every sin I'd ever commit before I drew my first breath. May I never lose my awe of your great love for me, and the reconciliation that was mine so long before I asked for it. I often don't feel I deserve this blessing, God, and how awesome that this truth doesn't change a thing. So, I bring my sins before you, asking for what is already mine, not out of need, but out of gratitude, respect, and love. Lord, being reconciled to you is a gift so great, I cannot hope to repay it. But with your help, I will live for you all my days.

Have you brought your sins to Jesus even though you may not feel you deserve his forgiveness?

Beauty in Pain

"In the same way I will not cause pain
without allowing something new to be born," says the LORD.
"If I cause you the pain, I will not stop you from giving birth
to your new nation," says your God.

ISAIAH 66:9 NCV

Lord, I know you are always faithful, always for me.
Even when there is pain, you can create a beautiful
outcome. But still I struggle with this, God. Why does
it have to hurt at all? Why can't I skip this part, the
suffering, and go straight to the reward? I don't
expect an answer. I just want to share my heart with
you honestly, trusting you'll bring me some comfort.
Perhaps the assurance that it will end, or the promise
that like a woman in labor, as I suffer, something
wonderful—and so worth the pain—is being born.
As I long for relief, let me rest in that promise.

**Are you in pain? Do you know that God can bring
something wonderful from it?**

Already Won

"The LORD your God is the one who goes with you to fight
for you against your enemies to give you victory."
DEUTERONOMY 20:4 NIV

Lord, you are always with me. Any threat to my
joy is an enemy of yours, which means it doesn't
stand a chance. Thank you for being at the front of
every battle I face. Please forgive me for occasionally
doubting our victory. I don't mean to rush out in
impatience or to retreat in fear, but sometimes I let
my focus travel from you to the enemy. Anger or
intimidation takes over, and I myself put the victory
in jeopardy. When I charge ahead of you, sword
flying and shield down, thank you for making sure
no arrow touches me or my children. When I cower
in fear, thank you, Lord, for your patience and gentle
reassurance. The battle is already won. Victory is ours.

Do you believe that the Lord your God is victorious?

Carrying Enough

"What does it profit them if they gain the whole world,
but lose or forfeit themselves?"
LUKE 9:25 NRSV

God, you hold everything in your hands, and yet you give all your attention to my cries for help. Amazing! Even the best juggler in the world eventually has too many moving objects and they crash to the ground, but you never drop a thing. No earnest prayer goes unheard. I'd ask you to help me better juggle my burdens, but I know you have a better solution. Father, help me know when I'm already carrying enough, and when I may need to set a few things down. Don't let me become all about my endless chores, schedules, and meetings; life is so much sweeter when I'm all about you.

Are you carrying too much? Do you need to set some things down?

Defeat Is Impossible

Then you will prosper, if you take care to fulfill the statutes and judgments with which the LORD charged Moses concerning Israel. Be strong and of good courage; do not fear nor be dismayed.

1 CHRONICLES 22:13 NKJV

Lord, what is it like to win every single time—to know going into the contest that you cannot lose? I have to admit something: I am afraid of defeat. I'm afraid of looking weak, of getting hurt, of not knowing where to go afterward. Father, give me your assurance that defeat is impossible, and I have nothing to fear. Even if things don't work out the way I want, I'll have avoided all the wasted hours of worry and doubt, and my confidence—your confidence—will reassure me that what seems like loss is actually part of the plan, that my victory is still ahead. I am looking for your assurance, Lord. This fear is getting heavy, and I'm ready to set it aside.

How can you make a point of setting your fear aside?

As I Know It

The world and its desires pass away,
but whoever does the will of God lives forever.
1 JOHN 2:17 NIV

Eternal Lord, I think of the whole span of my life,
eternity as I know it, and know it's just the tiniest
fraction of time to you. It's hard to grasp, and to be
honest, I'm not even sure I want to comprehend it.
Sometimes I grow weary and have grown to embrace
the idea that all things end. The idea of doing
anything forever is intimidating! But then I remember
your goodness, your absolute perfection. You would
not intend something that wasn't utterly wonderful.
I suspect I am intimidated only because I am here—
on this side of eternity, where nothing can satisfy.
Though I cannot grasp it, my heart knows it will be
fully satisfied with you on the other.

Isn't it wonderful to think that if you do God's will, you will live forever?

Matching Wisdom

"With God are wisdom and might;
he has counsel and understanding."
JOB 12:13 ESV

Wise Father, before I even ask for advice, you've prepared it. Before I even know to ask for help, you've made the way straight for me. You always know what I need. You always know what is best. Though I can't say why, I continually look elsewhere—as if there were anyone, anywhere, who could match your wisdom. Your patience, too, is unequaled. Lord, remind me to seek your counsel above all, and please continue to forgive me when I look to others first. You've proven I can trust you over and over, yet I continue to put my trust in the world. Make me wise enough to know yours is the only true wisdom, and to place my faith in only you.

Is it hard to put your faith only in God?

Each Holy Act

Pursue peace with everyone, and the holiness
without which no one will see the Lord.
HEBREWS 12:14 NRSV

Holy Lord, is there a description more like you, and less like anyone else, than "holy"? You are entirely perfect: without sin, without flaw. Every time I try to live a sinless day, I have failed before making breakfast. Still, the trying brings me closer to you, so I persist. I pursue you in your holiness. Oh, Holy Spirit, thank you for the help you give when I move aside and let you rule my heart! To love as you love and do as you do is the deepest desire of my heart. Each holy act of generosity, peace, and kindness brings me nearer to you, which is where I long to be.

What is the deepest desire of your heart?

It Will Be Done

I also persevered in the work on this wall, and we acquired no land, and all my servants were gathered there for the work.
NEHEMIAH 5:16 ESV

God, your perseverance gives me hope. You're always moving, never stopped; always progressing, never surrendered. Once you've begun a work, you finish it. I'd like to say the same for myself, but it gets overwhelming, and sometimes I want nothing more than to stop. The cooking, cleaning, washing, and constant responsibilities all get to be too much, and I think maybe I should give up. But that's not really what I want, of course. I don't want to stop; what I want is to finish. Help me persevere, Lord! Through fatigue, disappointment, setbacks, and even temporary failure, help me persevere. Remind me we are in this together, and because of that, it will all get done.

How can you persevere because of your hope in God?

Born of Pain

"This is My commandment, that you love one another,
just as I have loved you."
JOHN 15:12 NASB

Jesus, how did you set yourself aside for such ungrateful, undeserving sinners as myself? I want to be selfless, and sometimes I get close. An aching back and blistered feet go unnoticed in light of a joyful face, eyes spilling with gratitude, accepting your gift of love born of that momentary pain. It is in these moments that I am most in awe of your unfathomable love for us. I think of the times I am too proud, too willful, or too ashamed to meet your eyes, and the gift born of your pain compels me to my knees. Thank you, Jesus, for your perfect, selfless heart of love.

Do you know that Jesus loves you?

Beautiful Reflection

One thing I ask from the LORD, this only do I seek:
that I may dwell in the house of the LORD all the days of my life,
to gaze on the beauty of the LORD and to seek him in his temple.
PSALM 27:4 NIV

Beautiful God, to think that the most magnificent sunset, exquisite flower, or child's smile is just a tiny reflection of your beauty, I can't imagine it. But oh, how I long to see it! Just for a moment, I'd love to try to take it in. As I imagine it now, it makes me wonder why I would waste even a second looking at anything that is not from you. How do darkness and ugliness sometimes capture my attention? Take away my taste for that which is not beautiful, Lord! I want to spend all my time pursuing your goodness and glory, and not another moment on images or recreations that do not inspire, build, or beautify the lovely world you made for us.

Have you gazed on the beauty of the Lord lately?

My Safety

They will not be disgraced in hard times;
even in famine they will have more than enough.
PSALM 37:19 NLT

God, in times of trouble, I rely on your faithfulness. Problems mount on top of problems, building a bridge to get to me, but you are my safety. Therefore, I will not despair, no matter how high the pressure climbs. I know the only way for the enemy to reach me is for me to leave your safe shore, so I will remain. Lord, quiet my soul. I trust in your deliverance, but I am not untouched by these difficulties. I am pelted by grief, pain, and worry. I need to hear your song, to feel your arms around me, to be reminded of how the story ends.

Do you need to be reminded how the story ends?

Accept the Waiting

"Then you will call upon Me and go and pray to Me,
and I will listen to you."
JEREMIAH 29:12 NKJV

Lord, I know you hear me. Your ears are tuned to the prayers of the hearts that are surrendered to you. As soon as you hear me say your name, you are listening. You've already decided how and when to respond, and that response—and its timing—are perfect. While I wait, grant me the peace, the certainty, the surrender I need to accept the waiting. I grow impatient, not able to see all you see and know how beautifully the story ultimately goes. Come alongside me, God, and reassure me: this ends well! It ends just as it should, entirely for the good of myself and my family.

How can you know that God listens to you?

Thankful in Trials

My brothers and sisters, whenever you face trials of any kind,
consider it nothing but joy, because you know that t
he testing of your faith produces endurance;
and let endurance have its full effect, so that you
may be mature and complete, lacking in nothing.
JAMES 1:2–4 NRSV

Lord, I'm learning that when I walk with you, even the hard things are good things. Each time I face a trial, I have you as my defender. I learn a new facet of your great compassion and provision every time you bring me through. We grow closer, and I grow stronger. Lord, thank you for trials. I never thought I'd say that, but it's true; I thank you, because the more I face, the more I understand how you shape me and share yourself with me through them. As long as you are with me, bring it on! I can't wait to know more of you—and become a better me for my children.

Are you becoming better through your trials?

Where You Are

"Where two or three are gathered in my name,
there am I among them."
MATTHEW 18:20 ESV

Jesus, you said you'd be there when we come together in your name, and you are. There is something so beautiful about a friendship based on faith, something so sacred about gathering for the purpose of pursuing you. God, I love to meet with people who adore you. I know you must love it, too, because you are always there. There's a love intrinsic to Christian friendship that could only be from you: it transcends age, economics, and worldly interests; it goes straight to the heart of things, which is where we find you. Help me to foster an environment of believing in you so my children and I can meet together and experience your presence with us.

Isn't it wonderful that Jesus said he would be with us when we gather together in his name?

May

I pray that your hearts will be flooded with light so that you can understand the confident hope he has given to those he called—his holy people who are his rich and glorious inheritance.

EPHESIANS 1:18 NLT

A Glimpse

Surely there is a future,
And your hope will not be cut off.
PROVERBS 23:18 NASB

God of promise, please show me what to do with my disappointment. It's so hard, having your heart set on something, praying for it with confidence and belief, and being told no. I want to see it as not yet, or not that (because you have something better in mind). But in the moment, all I can hear is the no, and it hurts. It hurts my ears, and it hurts my heart. I need a glimpse down the path, Father. Would you lift me up on your shoulders, just for a moment, so I can see that where we are headed is indeed better than the road I wanted to take.

Do you need a glimpse down the path? Can you see that God has a future for you?

Captives Set Free

We have freedom now, because Christ made us free.
So stand strong. Do not change and go back
into the slavery of the law.
GALATIANS 5:1 NCV

Gracious Lord, you set captives free. However,
when we become ensnared, you offer a way out
and a room in the Father's house. Do you marvel
at our hesitation to accept? Thanks to your
redeeming love, the door to my own jail cell is wide
open and the guard is long gone, yet I still return to
it, crouching in the dirty corners as if that's where
I belong. Nevertheless, you find me there, every
time, and call me back to the freedom of your love,
back to my real home. Thank you for pulling me out
of darkness, and for your patience as I become
accustomed to the light.

How are you walking in your freedom through Christ?

All I Carry

"The foreigner residing among you must be treated
as your native-born. Love them as yourself,
for you were foreigners in Egypt. I am the LORD your God."
LEVITICUS 19:34 NIV

Generous God, you share all that is yours with me
and my children. Despite your example, my fists
remain clasped around what I can hold, my arms
encircling what I don't wish to share—just like a child
who holds onto that prized possession if only to keep
someone else from delighting in it. Open me up, Lord.
Remind me all I have is a blessing from you, and it's
meant to be shared. Thank you for children who test
me, needing more than I want to give, asking for more
than I am comfortable sharing. Pry my fingers away
from my palms and let me know the freedom of an
open hand. Fling open my arms, so all I try to carry
falls away, and I am available to wrap them around the
little people you've brought me to love.

What are you carrying that you need to let go of?

Enemies Will See

"Blessed are those who are persecuted for righteousness'
sake, for theirs is the kingdom of heaven."
MATTHEW 5:10 NKJV

Jesus, when I think of the persecution you faced for speaking the truth, for healing, and for pointing the way to the Father, it breaks my heart. When I realize there are people right this very minute suffering for those same reasons, I am moved to call out to you on their behalf. As lovers of your soul sit in chains, suffering beatings and worse, surround them with your presence, Lord! Send your Holy Spirit to give them a peace that completely transcends their situation. Let their enemies see the beauty of a life that is fully surrendered to you, and let their hearts be broken.

Who can you pray for that is being persecuted?

Within the Walls

> "Peace be within your walls,
> and security within your towers."
> PSALM 122:7 NRSV

Father, you are my protector. I scramble to acquire the position, possessions, and power to make me safe, but only with you am I truly secure. Let me know this, Lord, in the deepest part of my heart. Reveal my striving as mere running on a wheel. Security comes only from you. Regardless of the height of my tower or the size of my stockpile, outside of you, I am hiding in plain sight. But under your protection, even if my tower falls, I won't be harmed. Even if my body breaks, even if this life ends, with you my heart is at peace; my soul is secure.

Is your heart at peace and secure with your heavenly Father?

Inside Out

"Don't judge by his appearance or height, for I have rejected him. The LORD doesn't see things the way you see them. People judge by outward appearance, but the LORD looks at the heart."

1 SAMUEL 16:7 NLT

Lord, though Scripture tells us Jesus was nothing special to look at, I can only picture his as the most beautiful face anyone has ever seen. Beauty pours from his heart so powerfully it's blinding. Is that how you see, Father? From the inside out? How do I look? I care about my appearance, Lord. I admit it. I spend time and money presenting the best image I can to the world, but if you turned me inside out, what then? Please do it, Father. Flip me around so I see what matters to you. I want to invest in the image you see.

Do you know the Lord sees you from the inside out?

When We Doubt

Have mercy on those who doubt.
JUDE 1:22 ESV

Lord, how it must grieve you when we doubt. Scripture is filled with your faithfulness, power, and promise. Still, we question. We wonder, are you really there? Will you really come through? We know you are great, but we doubt you'll deliver. Or worse, when things get dark, we start to wonder if maybe we made the whole thing up. Nothing can last; no earthly love can truly satisfy. It's what we are used to, so we project it onto you. But you are so gracious, God, that you stick with us even then. You keep proving yourself, no matter how many times we ask it of you. In your mercy, you take that projection of doubt and bounce it back as blessed assurance.

What are you doubting? Can you believe for God's mercy?

Fear No Evil

Even though I walk through the valley of the shadow of death,
I fear no evil, for You are with me;
Your rod and Your staff, they comfort me.
PSALM 23:4 NASB

God, because of you, I have nothing to fear. Evil itself cannot harm me. Sin is unable to take hold of me. I wonder if I believe this? To be honest, I hope to never test it. Considering how terrifying an unexpected sound in the dark can be, I expect I'd experience my fair share of quaking and trembling if confronted with evil itself. But you know this, don't you? That is why you gave the reassurance of your Word. I will become afraid, but I don't have to stay there. Evil is nothing to you, so I will not fear for you are with me. Help me to show this truth to my children by encouraging them to walk closely with you so they never have to be afraid.

Do you know in your heart that you have nothing to fear because God is with you?

My Inspiration

All Scripture is given by inspiration of God,
and is profitable for doctrine, for reproof, for correction,
for instruction in righteousness.
2 TIMOTHY 3:16 NKJV

God, your Word is a lifeline! No matter what I face, question, or celebrate, the inspired words of Scripture provide what I need. The life in its pages inspires me to live mine more fully, more honestly, and with more love. Thank you! Lord, increase my desire for your Word, and deepen my understanding of its mysteries. Convict me of anything that grieves your heart and open me to the love that knows no limits. Let it be the source of all my inspiration, so my words and actions will bring pleasure and glory to you. Make this desire contagious so my children also desire to spend time in your Word learning more about your character and your goodness.

Who is the source of your inspiration?

All I Am

"Love the LORD your God with all your heart,
all your soul, and all your strength."
DEUTERONOMY 6:5 NCV

Lord, you hold nothing back from those who are committed to you. All the power in the world is at my disposal, once I stop relying on my own. Love itself can live in me if I'll only give it room. I don't know how my priorities get so off balance, God, but the beauty of your soul always draws me back. You ask a lot—all I am—but in return, you offer all you are. How can I refuse? Here's my soul, Father. Infuse it with your wisdom and grace. All my strength, my effort, my might, I want to expend in serving you. And please, have my heart, Lord. Empty it of all that is unloving; I want it overflowing with you.

Have you exchanged all of you for all of God?

You Get Me

We do not have a high priest who is unable to empathize with our weaknesses, but we have one who has been tempted in every way, just as we are—yet he did not sin.
HEBREWS 4:15 NIV

God, you understand temptation; you know weakness. You came to the earth as a man, and you felt hunger and pain. You experienced temptation. You know my struggle; you've resisted the pull of comfort and sacrificed the pleasure of the fleeting in exchange for the satisfaction of eternal. You get me. It's such a gift, Lord, to be able to approach you not with shame, but boldly, as one trying to overcome the very things you triumphed over. You don't judge me, though you have every right. You empathize, and you point the way past today, past my weakness, and to forever.

Aren't you glad that God understands temptation and that he has provided a way out?

Whole Again

The LORD is close to the brokenhearted;
he rescues those whose spirits are crushed.
PSALM 34:17 NLT

Precious Lord, the more we break, the closer you come. The cracks in us make space for you, and you fill that space with pure gold, making us whole again, but more beautiful, more valuable than before. A spirit crushed by the world has a chance to be reopened, expanded, and smoothed out. We are bigger and stronger for having borne the weight. Lord, I'm still a little fragile from the blows I've already taken. But I will thank you for the careful, loving, tender repairs you've made to this broken heart, this battered soul. I'll treasure your nearness as I trace the lines of my scars.

Are you brokenhearted or crushed? Do you know the Lord is close to you?

Empathy

Rejoice with those who rejoice, weep with those who weep.
ROMANS 12:15 NRSV

Lord, that you would choose to share my life, all the highs and lows, is such a miracle to me. To know you hurt when I'm hurting or when my children are hurting and laugh when we're laughing just does me in. How can we matter so much to you, knowing all too often we matter all too much to ourselves? Jealousy renders us unable to feel the joy of a friend who's just gotten something we want. Fear distances us from meeting them in their sorrow. Lord, open our hearts to the blessing of empathy! Help us to hurt with others when they experience grief and rejoice with them when they are full of joy.

Do you have someone you can rejoice or weep with today?

As It Should Be

If we know he hears us every time we ask him,
we know we have what we ask from him.
1 JOHN 5:15 NCV

Generous God, we ask, and you answer. Not every prayer, exactly as it is worded, but every pure intention, exactly as it should be. If I pray for a job interview to go my way, you know whether security, meaning, or even convenience is what my heart desires, and that is the prayer you answer.

If a relationship doesn't work despite many prayers, I know you have responded to the need I hoped that person would meet. Thank you, Lord, for knowing my heart. Your generosity is without exception or fault; your gifts are always good.

Do you know God hears you every time you speak to him?

Living on Camera

Whoever walks in integrity walks securely,
but he who makes his ways crooked will be found out.
PROVERBS 10:9 ESV

Father, do you laugh at us when we hide, like toddlers who think they can't be seen because they've covered their own eyes? You see me. You're right here. If I could see you next to me in the car, at the table, and especially alone with my thoughts, how differently would I behave? Holy Spirit, give me an awareness of your presence so tangible it's like I'm living on camera, broadcast to all of heaven and earth. I want to live a life of such integrity, no speech can hurt, and no action undermine my closeness with you, or the reputation of your church. If I am found out, let it be for my steadfast commitment to you. That is what I want my children to see and emulate.

How are you walking in integrity?

The Glorified Me

I know that I have not yet reached that goal,
but there is one thing I always do. Forgetting the past
and straining toward what is ahead.

PHILIPPIANS 3:13 NCV

Gracious Lord, before I sin, you forgive me. Please help me to forgive myself and lay regret aside. Your grace has no limit, and your focus is forward—on who I am becoming not who I used to be. You already see the glorified me, heir to the throne, and you long for the day I arrive. Regrets are cumbersome, making the journey clumsy and unnecessarily long. Help me accept the grace you offer without the burdens of regret and shame. Dwelling on my sin limits my progress toward completion. So, I look ahead to where you wait with my crown.

Are you looking ahead to your crown?

Father of Goodness

Praise the LORD in song, for He has done excellent things;
Let this be known throughout the earth.
ISAIAH 12:5 NASB

God, you are worthy. Praise, respect, honor, glory—all belong with you. With the help of your Spirit, let me find you in every good thing. As I marvel at talent, let me see the maker of the hands that did the painting, the architect of the voice who sang the song. As I behold beauty, let me see the mind who first conceived it. Let all my worship be directed at you, Lord. Let me honor the author of my faith, glorify the inventor of glory, and praise the Father of goodness. You alone are worthy, and I will worship you alone.

What excellent things has God done for you that you can proclaim to others?

Life Gets Busy

"Martha, Martha," the Lord answered, "you are worried
and upset about many things, but few things are needed—
or indeed only one. Mary has chosen what is better,
and it will not be taken away from her."
LUKE 10:41–42 NIV

Wise Lord, can I sit awhile at your feet and rest?
I like the sense of importance busyness gives me;
I feel necessary, purposeful, and capable, but I've
taken on so much, I'm not sure I am capable, and
my purpose has gotten a little unclear. In my desire
to be needed, I fear I've forgotten what I need. God,
grant me perspective. Life gets busy, especially
with children, and that can be good; there are little
people to love and tasks to accomplish and even the
occasional race to be run, but remind me to take time
to replenish, Lord. Remind me I am important because
you love me, not because of how much I get done.

Are you ready to sit and listen to Jesus?

With You

We can confidently say,
"The LORD is my helper;
I will not fear;
what can man do to me?"
HEBREWS 13:6 ESV

All-powerful God, what is too hard for you? And with you, what is too hard for me? With you next to me, I am strengthened. With you behind me, I am fortified. With you in front of me, I am shielded. With you holding me up, I am immovable. With you inside me, I know all this to be true. You give me confidence, Lord, and with that confidence, success. It doesn't matter who comes against me; it doesn't matter what they say, or do, or bring to defeat me. I have you, and you've got me. Help me to demonstrate this truth to my children, so they are also confident in your strength and protection.

What is too hard for you? Is it too hard for God?

Stay in the Fight

The godly may trip seven times, but they will get up again.
But one disaster is enough to overthrow the wicked.
PROVERBS 24:16 NLT

Unfailing Lord, each time I fall, you're there to pick me up. The gentle way you set me back on my feet inspires me to try again, no matter how many times I fail. Until I give up, it isn't over and until you're not there to lift me, I'm staying in the fight. Thank you, Father, for always being there. You take what looks like failure and show it to me as a step in my progress. Each time I fall I learn more about how to stand; each time you pick me up, I learn more about your limitless faithfulness.

Did you trip again? Do you know God was there to pick you up?

Absent of Judgment

"Do not judge, and you will not be judged;
do not condemn, and you will not be condemned.
Forgive, and you will be forgiven."
LUKE 6:37 NRSV

Lord God, you are the only rightful judge. Only you see into our hearts, past the lies we tell, the masks we wear, and the scars handed down through generations. Forgive me for the times I borrow your gavel, thinking I know who someone is though I can't possibly know their heart. My opinion does nothing to influence your verdict of them, but it may very well seal your decision regarding my fate. I'm sorry, Father. I have no business hurling stones at anyone. Remake my heart in the image of Jesus: absent of judgment, void of condemnation, and overflowing with forgiveness.

Is your heart overflowing with forgiveness?

Honored

If anyone does not provide for his own,
and especially for those of his household, he has denied
the faith and is worse than an unbeliever.

1 TIMOTHY 5:8 NASB

God, the way you provide for your children is awesome. You are so specifically attentive to each of us who calls you Father; nothing slips through the cracks. In my own life, I rarely succeed in giving proper attention to all the responsibilities you've entrusted to me. Inevitably, I get distracted or wrapped up in myself, and I need forgiveness—from my children and from you—yet again. Lord, plant in me a fresh commitment to my commitments. May the children you've given me to love and the things you have given me to do take precedence over every temptation and every distraction. Help me to honor what you have honored me with, God, so I can honor you.

Who or what is distracting you from what God wants you to do?

A Break from Striving

"My presence will go with you, and I will give you rest."
EXODUS 33:14 ESV

Ever-present God, just to remember you are always with me slows the frantic pace of my heart. I don't need to keep running, keep looking over my shoulder, keep striving past exhaustion. You are with me; I cannot fail! It's okay to close my eyes, because yours are always open. Thank you, Lord, for keeping watch over my life so I can rest. No harm will come to me while I take time to restore my strength. You won't allow it. When I take a break from all my striving, I find you here, waiting, with all I need to keep going. When I slow down and meet with you, I am renewed.

Have you taken time to rest in God's presence?

Lesser Things

Let what you heard from the beginning abide in you.
If what you heard from the beginning abides in you,
then you will abide in the Son and in the Father.
1 JOHN 2:24 NRSV

Lord, your Word is alive, and I want it to live in me.
When I make my heart a home for the things you've
taught me, peace rules my life. When I crowd out your
truth with the things of this world, I am controlled
by chaos, confusion, and dissatisfaction. That I
allow this to happen is confounding; why would I
choose anything over the peace of abiding with you?
Holy Spirit, I need your presence; otherwise, I am
an empty vessel, prone to the enemy's schemes to
distract me. I want you to take up every inch of my
heart and mind—leave no room for lesser things.
Abide in me, so I can abide in the Father.

Have you left room for lesser things?

Better Than Winning

When you do things, do not let selfishness or pride
be your guide. Instead, be humble and give more honor
to others than to yourselves.
PHILIPPIANS 2:3 NCV

Perfect Lord, even as a man, you could have won every contest, silenced every argument, ended every debate. Your limitless ability and brilliance made you undefeatable, but that wasn't why you came. It's not why I'm here, either, is it? I don't behave as though I know this; forgive me. Lord, help me remember that just because I can win, doesn't mean I need to. Show me that most of my life is not a competition at all. Remind me that building my children and others up and seeing their success often feels even better than winning, and it's far more pleasing to you.

Are you competing with someone instead of building them up?

Increase My Faith

The apostles said to the Lord, "Increase our faith."
LUKE 17:5 NLT

God, no matter how much faith I have, it will never be too much. So often I fear it is far from enough. I know you are good. I know you are capable of great miracles, and you love to astonish us. Still, I limit you by limiting my prayers. I don't ask for what you might not choose to give. Forgive me and increase my faith. On the days I doubt, the days I fear, the days I hesitate to ask for what I know you would love to give me, increase my faith, Lord. Tell me to test you by asking boldly, by believing wholeheartedly, then astonish me by responding with your perfect love.

How might you be limiting the Lord by your lack of faith?

This Unmerited Favor

Sin shall not have dominion over you,
for you are not under law but under grace.
ROMANS 6:14 NKJV

God, how do I thank you for grace? How do I even comprehend it? It is too much, this unmerited favor, for my mind to grasp. No matter what I've done, I am forgiven. No sin can claim me, because you already have. Even as I accept this, I am still blown away by the unfairness of it: your favor is unmerited yet bestowed on me extravagantly. What I am is yours, and that is all that matters. Sin invites me to choose the law, to take my chances with acts and actions, but you invite me home—right into the arms of grace.

Are you living as though you are under the law or grace?

Yet You Stay

All my longings lie open before you, LORD;
my sighing is not hidden from you.
PSALM 38:9 NIV

Lord, you meet me in my loneliness and turn it to joy. In those moments when I feel alone, I can always draw into you. When I am by myself, your presence fills me with wholeness. When I am surrounded by others but am feeling misunderstood, or alone in my convictions, your presence fills me with belonging. You see me, even when no one else does. To know you see me—right to my unuttered thoughts—fulfills my deepest longing, to be both understood and accepted. You know me, and yet you stay, always. To be so loved as that leaves no room for loneliness.

Have you laid your longings before the Lord, so he can fill them with his love?

Lessen My Grip

Do not forget to do good and to share,
for with such sacrifices God is well pleased.
HEBREWS 13:16 NKJV

Lord, I know because of Jesus, we no longer need to prove our devotion or be forgiven for our sins through sacrifice. Still, to give back to you some of what you've so generously given to me feels good and right. I want to please you, Lord, and I know you love a generous heart. God, help me lessen my grip on my time, and help me to loosen my concept of what's mine. I see this quality in others and it is beautiful to behold. Their selfless acts remind me how much more generous I could be, if only I'd open my hand. Grant me a heart that shares what's been given to me, one that gives more than I think it can.

What are you holding on to that you need to let go of?

Unconditional Acceptance

"All that the Father gives Me will come to Me, and the one who comes to Me I will certainly not cast out."
JOHN 6:37 NASB

Precious Lord, in a world where acceptance is a rare commodity, elusive even among loved ones, your unconditional acceptance of me is a gift I treasure. The day I accepted your gift of eternal life, you accepted me—and all my imperfections—forever. I'm inspired, Lord, to be unconditional in my love toward my children. But I am weak, imperfect. This causes me to judge, to hold a grudge, to withhold what was not withheld from me. Holy Spirit, don't let me do it! Remind me of the acceptance I have in Christ and demand that I extend it to these important people in my life.

Is it hard for you to accept the fact that you are unconditionally loved by your heavenly Father?

Aim for Harmony

Let us aim for harmony in the church
and try to build each other up.
ROMANS 14:19 NLT

God, the beauty of music tells me how much you love harmony. The sounds of voices and instruments working together, creating a beautiful sound, bring you praise and draw you nearer while the sounds of argument and dissent distance us from you. Instead of arguing, let me compromise when the outcome will be peace. I want to be close to you, God, always. When I am tempted to argue, to add to the cacophony of noise that drives you away, let a song of praise fill my thoughts. Let the melody wash over me until I remember that compromise is harmony, and harmony is worship. Let all my interactions be as harmonious as a symphony.

How can you interact with God's people to help build them up and cause harmony?

June

"Whatever you ask in prayer,
believe that you have received it,
and it will be yours."

MARK 11:24 ESV

Dependable

Let not steadfast love and faithfulness forsake you;
bind them around your neck;
write them on the tablet of your heart.
PROVERBS 3:3 ESV

Faithful God, your reliability is solid; I build my life on its foundation. If only my gratitude for your unwavering commitment to me gave me the same faithfulness toward these children you've given me to love. I let them down, Lord, and it grieves me to grieve them. I want faithfulness to pour from me as naturally as water from a spring. It matters to you, God. I know, because of how prominently you display your own. Let me be dependable as you are dependable, committed as you are committed. Lord, let my faithfulness be set in stone.

Are you dependable and committed?

I Will Rejoice

This is the day the LORD has made;
We will rejoice and be glad in it.
PSALM 118:24 NKJV

Lord, I want to be grateful for every day, but
circumstances sometimes make it feel impossible.
How do I rejoice when I am grieving or in danger?
Where's the gladness in a day of sorrow or plight?
Help me find it, Holy Spirit! When I cannot see what
to celebrate, invade my thoughts with your incredible
love. Don't let the moments of compassion, rescue,
and comfort go unnoticed. Make me glad for a
chance to depend on you. Let me rejoice when I
experience your peace, most especially on a day
when there is no peace around me. Remind me that
every day—every single day—contains the joy of
the Lord.

Do you believe that this can be an amazing day filled
with the joy of the Lord?

With All

"Love the LORD your God with all your heart,
all your soul, all your strength, and all your mind."
Also, "Love your neighbor as you love yourself."
LUKE 10:27 NCV

God, Jesus gave all for me. That's how much you love me—how much you love my children. And it's how much you want us to love you. Jesus came to show us how to live, and he lived a life of utter devotion to you and to us, your children. Thank you for showing us such a wonderful love. Fill my heart, making all my desires in line with your will. Take my soul for your own; I want to worship only you. Use my strength to build your kingdom. Shape my mind through your Word. Let me see my children's comfort and safety as important as my own. I want to give you all.

Have you given your all?

Every Moment

Teach us to number our days,
that we may gain a heart of wisdom.
PSALM 90:12 NIV

Wise Father, let me learn from you. More than anything, teach me to value the hours. I want to make the most of the time you've given me, but day after day, my good intentions drift by in a sea of distraction—or are carried off on waves of willful rebellion. I say this is not what I want, but it is what I do, again and again. Give me a wise heart, Father. Wise enough to know that every moment is a gift, deserving of gratitude and intention. The plans you have for me are good. I want to cooperate with you each moment of the day.

Are you making the most of each day?

All Grace

After you suffer for a short time, God, who gives all grace, will make everything right. He will make you strong and support you and keep you from falling. He called you to share in his glory in Christ, a glory that will continue forever.
1 PETER 5:10 NCV

Lord, why must we suffer? I'm not going to pretend to be okay with it today, God, because it's just too hard. It hurts! To see parents grieve the loss of their child, or to hear of an innocent victim of an unspeakable crime, my heart aches as if the pain were my own—and I can only ask why. These are the times, Lord, where I want to see what you see, knowing when suffering will end, and the age of constant rejoicing will begin. Until then, I rely on your strength. Give me all the grace I need. You will keep me from falling and make everything right.

Where do you need God's grace today?

Humble Help

If another believer is overcome by some sin, you who are godly should gently and humbly help that person back onto the right path. And be careful not to fall into the same temptation yourself.
GALATIANS 6:1 NLT

God, yours are the only standards. Help us to live by them alone. When I am in the wrong, give me the kind of friends who will hold me accountable. And when I am aware of the sin of a sister or brother, grant me the confidence and conviction— not of my own righteousness, but of yours—to do the same. Holy Spirit, I cannot do this without you. It is so much easier to tolerate transgression, to worry about just my own sins, but you ask for more than that. When I need it, fill me with the conviction, gentleness, and humility to hold those I love accountable. And let me do so in a way that honors both them and you.

Who can you humbly and gently help today?

Before Confessing

If we confess our sins, he who is faithful and just will
forgive us our sins and cleanse us from all unrighteousness.
1 JOHN 1:9 NRSV

God, you know all my sins before I even act. You
forgave me for them all before I was born. All you
ask in return is that I bring them before you. Before I
can confess, I must be aware. And once I am aware,
I must be sorry. I need your help with both; I cannot
trust my own heart. Show me all my sins, so nothing
remains unconfessed. Without a mirror, or a friend,
I may never know of the dirt on my face. Without
your Word and the conviction of your Holy Spirit,
I could never know all the ways I am indebted to
your forgiveness. Show me, cleanse me, and let me
thank you!

**Do you have sins that need to be confessed and
forgiven?**

We Are Family

I bow my knees before the Father, from whom
every family in heaven and on earth is named.
EPHESIANS 3:14–15 ESV

God, you are Father to us all. When I think of how deep the love of a good earthly father runs, and when I remember that this is a mere fraction of the depth of your love for every single one of us, my knees weaken. We are family, you and I, along with everyone else who has ever lived. I can scarcely take this in. Father, help me properly cherish the family you've given me. No matter the quarrels and disappointments, I love them. They love me. At the end of the day, it's the closest I can come here on earth to you, which makes them the most precious gift I have. Thank you.

Do you cherish the family God has given you?

My Deepest Pain

"Blessed are those who mourn, for they shall be comforted."
MATTHEW 5:4 NASB

Lord, it comforts me to know you are always wise, always good, always for me, especially in my grief. You said we are blessed when we mourn. It's confounding to those who have never known loss—or known it with you as their comforter—but to me, it is beautiful truth. Only in my deepest pain do I grasp the depth of your love. That I could feel even a minute of joy while suffering the loss of someone I loved so dearly was a gift so sweet, it could only have come from you. That I could believe in my great sadness I would ever be happy again was a testament to the comforting power of your love. Thank you for being there.

Are you mourning? Do you need the Lord's comfort today?

Pay It Forward

Judgment will be without mercy to anyone who has
shown no mercy; mercy triumphs over judgment.

JAMES 2:13 NRSV

Merciful God, how do you do it? No matter how
little we deserve it, you show us mercy, give us yet
another chance—and then another. My own mercy
gets worn thin. How many second chances do I have
to give, how many times should I count to three? I'm
going to need your help with this one too. Be merciful
toward my unmerciful heart; change it for the better.
Give me your inexhaustible patience and grace so
I can show endless mercy to my children and to
others just as it's been shown to me. How better can
I thank you than to pay mercy forward? Show me
how and let your mercy triumph in my life.

How did you see God's mercy toward you today?

You Are Security

"Behold, I will bring to it health and healing,
and I will heal them and reveal
to them abundance of prosperity and security."
JEREMIAH 33:6 ESV

God, you are security. When I place my hope in the things of this world: money, achievement, acceptance, and health, I am bound to insecurity. None of those things—or in all this world—are guaranteed. Nothing lasts. There is no security, except in the one who never changes, the one who cannot fail, the one who is love itself. Let my health be in my soul, my achievement be for your kingdom, my acceptance be at your table, and my riches be treasures in heaven. I'm placing all my hope in you, that it may be secure.

Have you placed all your security in God?

For Your Glory

> "Seek first His kingdom and His righteousness,
> and all these things will be added to you."
> MATTHEW 6:33 NASB

God, no accomplishment is beyond you. Your greatness inspires me to greatness. I see the brilliance of creation, and of your children, and I long to accomplish something great. I know you gave me this ambition, that it is holy at its most pure. I also know the enemy wants nothing more than to twist what is holy. Help me keep my ambition pure, Lord! Give me a desire to see your purpose revealed and fulfilled that drowns out all other goals. If I desire greatness, make it greatness for your glory. If I long for fame, make it be for shining a light on yours. Use my ambition to accomplish yours, God.

What great accomplishment does God want to do in your life?

Reason for Success

The LORD will be your confidence,
And will keep your foot from being caught.
PROVERBS 3:26 NASB

God, you are the author of my confidence. Any talent or goodness I possess is from you. I confess I sometimes gain my sense of self from my attributes instead of from you, who made me as I am. I place my confidence in the intelligence or giftedness, rather than on you who bestowed it. Please forgive me. If I run without stumbling, it is because you are my agility. If I run the fastest, you are my speed. If I run the farthest, my endurance is you. You are my confidence, Lord. You are responsible for everything good about me, and you are every reason I succeed.

Is your confidence in the Lord?

My Parachute

When I am afraid,
I will put my trust in you.
PSALM 56:3 NLT

God who takes away fear, would you please take mine—again. I say I trust you with my life and with the lives of my children, and then the moment things get a little scary, I try to take it back from you. When I most need to surrender is when my hands are clenched the tightest. Help me to open them, to rest in your waiting arms. You are my parachute, Lord, yet I find I am too afraid to pull the cord. Forgive me for my lack of faith and prove to me—again—how silly I am, enduring this free fall when you are right beside me, waiting for me to let go, so you can carry me safely home.

Can you trust the Lord enough to be your parachute?

Bloom

Grow in the grace and knowledge of our Lord and Savior
Jesus Christ. To him be glory both now and forever! Amen.
2 PETER 3:18 NIV

God, grower of everything beautiful, help me to
bloom! If I were a plant, where would I be in my cycle
of growth? I know I'm no longer a seed, for I can
feel I've begun to grow. My roots have started to
spread and take hold as I've grown closer to you and
learned the truth in your Word. And I've felt the light
of the sun as I burst from the soil, a new life in you.
But beyond that, how far have I come? How close
am I to the beautiful flower you intended? Help me,
Father, to grow as tall, as deep, and as wide as you
have planned, then to bloom with all the color and
audacity I can.

Are you growing where you have been planted?

Thoughts Captured

Think about the things that are good and worthy of praise.
Think about the things that are true and honorable
and right and pure and beautiful and respected.
PHILIPPIANS 4:8 NCV

Dear Father, why do my thoughts so often take me captive, pulling me away from the moment? Even singing a familiar song of praise, my mind sometimes wanders. Instead of immersing myself in the joy of contemplating your goodness, I find I am either planning my day or rehashing my night. Help me to direct my thoughts to you. You are light and perfection, beauty and truth. This is how I want to spend my thought life: considering you and your glorious creation. I can't control what comes into my head, but I can learn to turn the tables, to capture my thoughts before they capture me. Help me, Lord, to master my mind. I turn my thoughts to you and to all that is good.

What thoughts of yours need to be captivated by the Lord?

Choose Your Way

A man without self-control
is like a city broken into and left without walls.
PROVERBS 25:28 ESV

Lord, you are sovereign. You could take control at any moment, yet you give me unlimited freedom. So that I learn self-control and come to you willingly, you do not interfere. I am a slow learner, Father. Forgive me for my lack of self-control. Precious Lord, I need your help. Show me how vulnerable I am when I ignore my convictions, compromise my integrity, and surrender to temptation. I'm leaving the door wide open, and the enemy is just waiting to storm through and take over my life. Remind me, Father, how much sweeter—and safer—it is to choose your way.

Which way have you chosen to go?

Good Sense

Those with good sense are slow to anger,
and it is their glory to overlook an offense.
PROVERBS 19:11 NRSV

Lord, your patience is great, your forgiveness overwhelming. I have no doubt I frustrate you, but you don't become angry with me. My own fuse can be short, and the resulting explosion something I am not proud of. Please forgive me for my anger. Help me to keep it in check, to not be so quickly offended when my child says or does something careless. You love it when I respond as you would. Give me your heart, Father—your endless patience. When I feel offended, turn my thoughts toward how often I have been granted grace. As I have received, let me give: grace upon grace. Give me good sense to overlook an offense.

Wouldn't it be great to overlook offenses and extend mercy?

Contentment

Each of you should continue to live in whatever
situation the Lord has placed you, and remain
as you were when God first called you.
1 CORINTHIANS 7:17 NLT

Lord, you numbered the hairs on my head, and
you notice when one falls. Your attention to my life
is so intricate, so loving. How can I question or
complain about my circumstances? Where I am is
where you placed me; what I have is what you gave.
Father, please forgive my restlessness and lack of
contentment. Help me, please, to live and be grateful
for my life, thankful for my children. I don't want
to chase after what others have. Help me to know
that I am here on purpose, as a result of your loving
intentions. Fill me with contentment, Lord, so I can
make the most of the life you chose for me.

What area is the hardest for you to be content in?

Ultimate Guide

Follow my example, as I follow the example of Christ.
1 CORINTHIANS 11:1 NIV

Lord, thank you for being a perfect leader. As a follower, I come up short time and again. But when I want to know how to get it right, I can always turn my attention back to you and to others who choose you as their leader. Thank you for the godly leaders you've placed in my life and thank you for being the ultimate guide. When I stray from the path, tempted and distracted by shiny, temporary things of this world, lead me back. When I am attracted to something that contradicts your teaching, turn my intrigue to revulsion. Lead me, Lord; I will follow.

Do you have someone who helps you turn your attention back to Jesus?

Nothing to Condemn

There is now no condemnation
for those who are in Christ Jesus.
ROMANS 8:1 NASB

Merciful, forgiving God, help me let go of my guilt and lay it at your feet. You forgave me long ago; it was easy for you. But Lord, I hate what I've done. I'm afraid if I forgive myself, I am excusing myself—and there is no excuse. Lord, help me know the difference between conviction and condemnation. Guilt and shame are not part of your plan for me. Help me let go of my old self, and to look back on my sins as if they were committed by someone else—because according to you, they were. In you I am new; there is nothing to condemn.

How do you know the difference between conviction and condemnation?

Never Too Big

"You don't have enough faith," Jesus told them. "I tell you
the truth, if you had faith even as small as a mustard seed,
you could say to this mountain, 'Move from here to there,'
and it would move. Nothing would be impossible."
MATTHEW 17:20 NLT

Lord God, mover of mountains, I'm standing at the
bottom of one right now. I know I believe you can,
but I'm not sure I believe you will. It seems too big,
the kind of thing you did ages ago, but not today. It
feels like the kind of miracle you'd work for someone
with more faith, or someone who has done more
for you. Help me with my unbelief, Lord! Move this
mountain, God. Fill me with confident hope. Take this
little mustard seed and water it. Let it grow in the
certainty—huge and full—that even today, in the
name of Jesus, you can and you do and you will.

What mountains do you need faith to remove?

Selflessness

Let each of you look out not only for his own interests,
but also for the interests of others.
PHILIPPIANS 2:4 NKJV

God, you are completely worthy of worship, yet
you spend all your time thinking of others while I,
who deserve no worship at all, spend most of my
time thinking of myself. I long for the freedom of
selflessness, but then realize that even that longing
is about me! When it comes to dying to self, I don't
even know where to begin. Father, remake me in
your image. Devotion to you looks like devotion to
my children, and I want to give you all my allegiance.
Give me a heart that is entirely focused on you and
other people. Take away all thoughts of me and
replace them with expressions of you.

Is your heart focused on Jesus and others?

Make You Proud

Do your best to present yourself to God as one approved by him, a worker who has no need to be ashamed, rightly explaining the word of truth.
2 TIMOTHY 2:15 NRSV

Father, I know I have your love and forgiveness; what I long for is your approval. Because you love me so perfectly, I want to make you proud. I want to be the child who is constantly looking for ways to honor you, who never needs reminding of the rules. Keep me close by, Lord, so I can hear your encouragements and heed your admonishments. Let me know your will instinctively and empower me by your Holy Spirit to act on it. Let me sense your presence, so I am encouraged to do and say only what will glorify you—not because I fear your anger, but because I love your approval.

Do you know that you have God's approval?

Take Courage

"Have I not commanded you? Be strong and of good courage;
do not be afraid, nor be dismayed, for the LORD your God is
with you wherever you go."
JOSHUA 1:9 NKJV

Lord, my courage comes entirely from you. To
face even a day without your protective presence
is unimaginable. What should be equally hard to
fathom is how I could possibly be afraid when you
are with me, but I grow fearful all too often. Forgive
my weakness, Father. Life gets heavy as threats and
challenges loom always before me. Fear waits for an
opportunity to pounce and takes it, leaving me pinned
beneath the weight. You witness it all, then gently
remind me of your presence. What power can hold
me down when faced with you? From this I take up
courage, lay hold of strength, and move forward—
boldly—into whatever awaits.

**How can you know that the Lord is with you wherever
you go?**

Forgive Me

Consider my affliction and my trouble,
and forgive all my sins.
PSALM 25:18 ESV

Merciful God, I've sinned—again—and I feel the distance it's creating between us. I fear I could pray this every day, and nothing would change. Why is it so hard to do what I want, which is to live in your will? My sins may be small, but each one adds to the chasm. Please forgive me, Father. I hate my sin; I hate the gulf it creates between our hearts, as I move toward darkness and you remain in the light. I want to be near you, to live in your presence, and to serve you. Nothing else compares, and I should know; I've tried it all. You are all I want, Lord. Please leave the light on! I'm coming home.

Do you believe that God will forgive you of all your sins?

A New Heart

"He who believes in Me, as the Scripture has said,
out of his heart will flow rivers of living water."
JOHN 7:38 NKJV

Savior, in your great love, you took my cold, selfish heart and replaced it with warmth and compassion. You gave me a new heart! Thoughts and actions I know could not have come from the old heart flow freely from this one. Where do I begin to repay such a debt? Thank you, Lord, for showing me how much there is to this life. Thank you for feelings of mercy, grace, generosity, and hope. Thank you for moments of completely forgetting myself as I am swept up in you. Thank you for opportunities to love the children you have placed in my care and to point them to the source of my radiance. Thank you for the new life of a new heart.

Are the rivers of living water flowing from your heart?

By Your Grace

"If you forgive those who sin against you,
your heavenly Father will forgive you. But if you refuse to
forgive others, your Father will not forgive your sins."
MATTHEW 6:14–15 NLT

Gracious God, the depth of your willingness to forgive shows me how close forgiveness is to your heart. Is there much you value more than when we extend your grace to someone who needs it? And when they don't deserve it, how much more do our forgiving hearts delight you? I need your help with this, Father. When I'm faced with an unforgivable offense, help me separate it from the offender. While actions may not always be redeemable, remind me that people always are. Help me recall that to withhold my forgiveness is to jeopardize yours. And when by your grace I've given grace, grant me the incomparable pleasure of your joyful presence.

Is there someone who needs you to extend grace or forgiveness?

How Much

"The very hairs of your head are all numbered."
MATTHEW 10:30 NKJV

God, you love me so perfectly; I come back to it again and again, and I still can't believe how much I matter to you. Every breath I take is significant; each hair on my head is numbered. You take account when they fall. You took on flesh and dealt with every hurt and temptation to understand me better, to atone for my sin. You died for me. It's too much, my significance to you, which is odd, because I strive so hard to matter here. I crave attention, grasp for accomplishments, and revel in accolades—none of which matters in comparison to what you, the God of the universe, did for me. Your great love humbles me utterly. Thank you, Father.

Do you realize how much you matter to God?

Joyful Surrender

"All authority in heaven and on earth has been given to me."
MATTHEW 28:18 NIV

Jesus, I recognize your authority over every living thing, and I marvel at how loosely you hold it. When you walked the earth, to consider how easily you could have brought everyone you encountered to submission—and the love and humility it took to lay that power aside—takes my breath away. You don't claim your authority; you wait for joyful surrender. I surrender, Lord. Accept my white flag and take control of my whole life. I trust your authority completely and my own not at all. Joyfully, I hand you my heart, my will, and my might. I am yours.

Have you joyfully surrendered everything to Jesus?

July

He will answer the prayers of the needy;
he will not reject their prayers.

PSALM 102:17 NCV

Deleting Criticism

Do not let any unwholesome talk come out of your mouths,
but only what is helpful for building others up according to
their needs, that it may benefit those who listen.
EPHESIANS 4:29 NIV

God, you are the only worthy critic, yet you offer only grace, acceptance, and love. Even when you are convicting me of sin, you do it in a way that I feel loved, not criticized. Let me learn from your example, Lord; kill my critical spirit. Just because I have a thought, doesn't mean I need to speak it. I may know a better way to go about something, but if sharing so would serve no good purpose, mute my lips. When I speak, let it be to build, not tear down—to encourage, not discourage. Help me shine light, Lord, not cast shadows. Pull criticism from my heart and replace it with unconditional love so my children and others around me know your love and encouragement.

Is your speech benefiting those who listen to you?

Your Reasons

Every man's way is right in his own eyes,
But the LORD weighs the hearts.

PROVERBS 21:2 NASB

Wise Father, what do you see when you search my heart? Are my intentions true, my motives pure? I think I am living for you, but I sometimes fear perhaps I live for the way you make me feel. Or I wonder if it's really you I am trying to impress, or the world who sees what I do or hears what I say in your name. Show me, Father, if my motives lack truth. Align my goals with your plans and make all my dreams for myself and my children the ones you give me. Motivate me, Lord, to want only good things and for only your reasons.

What does the Father see when he searches your heart?

While I Wait

Now they desire a better, that is, a heavenly country.
Therefore God is not ashamed to be called their God,
for He has prepared a city for them.
HEBREWS 11:16 NKJV

Father in heaven, I long for the day you establish your kingdom here. Everything good about the world—love, beauty, peace—will only get better, and everything dark will be gone. You can't come soon enough. I know you're preparing a place for me and for my children; I can't wait to see it. While I wait, Lord, let me give and receive love, create and experience beauty, inspire and dwell in peace. Help me satisfy my longing for heaven by improving the earth. Allow me, Father, to know you as well as I can and to show you to those you have placed in my care. As I wait for your kingdom to come to earth, let your Spirit come to my heart.

Are you excited about God's coming kingdom?

I Am Free

"Then you will know the truth,
and the truth will make you free."
JOHN 8:32 NCV

God, only the freedom you offer is truly free. When I choose to ignore your ways, and I am free to sin however and whenever I wish, the sin itself enslaves me. I invite something as seemingly inconsequential as gossip in the door and the next thing I know, envy, greed, and compromise have broken it down and taken me hostage. But with you am I free to move about, unencumbered by negative emotions and acts. Lord, thank you for inviting me to stand in your truth. You invite me to let your law, the law of love, rule my heart. I am free to accept, and when I accept, I am free.

Has the truth set you free?

Simplicity

I fear, lest somehow, as the serpent deceived Eve
by his craftiness, so your minds may be corrupted
from the simplicity that is in Christ.
2 CORINTHIANS 11:3 NKJV

Amazing God, you contain all the complexity of the universe, yet there is an unmatched simplicity to you as well. I complicate things by bringing in the world and all its trappings, but a life lived for you is really a simple thing. It's all love. One thing: what could be simpler than that? Lord, you ask so little of me—to live simply so I can love extravagantly. Why do I feel the need to make my assignment any bigger? Why do I listen to the lie that I need more? Because you are so good, even the solution is simple: slow down, step back, and love. I'll start today with this simple request: will you help me?

Are you living simply, so you can love extravagantly?

A Season

For everything there is a season,
and a time for every matter under heaven:
ECCLESIASTES 3:1 NRSV

Lord, you are perfect in wisdom and infallible with your timing. No wonder you can balance the whole world at once! Allow me to learn from you, God. When my life seems out of balance—which is almost always—remind me to consider your wisdom and your timing. Help me consider the season—to be wise enough to know what is needed and what can wait. Remind me too that balanced doesn't always mean even; one side of a scale can be much heavier than the other. But as long both are floating, there is balance. And as I teeter, trying to manage it all, comfort me with the image of your hand gently cradling me and keeping me afloat.

What season of life are you living in now? Can you see God?

Not Defeated

Every child of God defeats this evil world,
and we achieve this victory through our faith.
1 JOHN 5:4 NLT

Lord, your victory is assured. I cling to this hope in the face of my own defeat. Your power and your great love for me are all that keep me going some days, as life beats me down, tells me no, and hands my victories to someone else. Father, hold me tight and speak to me again—I need to hear it. It's hard not to give up when failure heaps upon loss, and loss piles upon disappointment. Remind me of your goodness and restore my faith in the bounce back, Lord. It may not feel like it today, but the victory is already won. I may be down, but I am not defeated. Tomorrow is coming, and tomorrow I win.

As tomorrow comes do you believe that you have the victory?

Willingly Tethered

Perfume and incense bring joy to the heart,
and the pleasantness of a friend
springs from their heartfelt advice.
PROVERBS 27:9 NIV

Gracious God, friend to all, how I thank you for the gift of friendship! Unlike family, where blood and history bind us, friends willingly tether themselves together. You chose my friends just for me; you sent us to one another, so we would feel chosen, special, "gotten." Forgive me for sometimes taking friendship for granted. I know how fortunate I am to be blessed with people who love me entirely for who I am. It's another way you give me a glimpse of your love and its many facets, and it's beautiful. Help me to value and honor my friends, Lord, for the treasures they are.

What special friendship has God given to you?

Whatever I Ask

"If in my name you ask me for anything, I will do it."
JOHN 14:14 NRSV

Lord Jesus, you promise to do whatever I ask in your name. I must confess I doubt this at times. After all, when two opponents both pray in your name for victory, one must always be disappointed. So how do I know when you will help me versus my opposition? Dear Lord, just to speak your name invites peace and confidence into my heart. The answer is so clear; you are always helping me, even when I don't get my way. To pray in your name is to pray surrendered to the Father, who is always working for my good, even when it is not to my immediate happiness. Thank you, Jesus, that my ultimate joy is always before you.

What are you asking Jesus for today?

Much Need

Even lions may get weak and hungry,
but those who look to the LORD will have every good thing.
PSALM 34:10 NCV

Lord, there is so much need! When I step outside myself and consider the depth of it, I am moved to tears—and overcome by helplessness. What can anyone do when there is so very much to be done? Where do I begin? Make me attentive to your answer, God. Pierce my heart until I cry out on their behalf. I know that you are listening, ready to move where you are invited. Keep me here, outside myself, and attuned to the things that break your heart. Holy Spirit, move me to ask the Father to move for them. And then, let me see him respond.

Are you looking to the Lord for an answer to all the needs around you?

Bearing Gifts

There are varieties of gifts, but the same Spirit.
And there are varieties of ministries, and the same Lord.
There are varieties of effects, but the same God who
works all things in all persons. But to each one is given
the manifestation of the Spirit for the common good.
1 CORINTHIANS 12:4–7 NASB

Lord, how I thank you for your Holy Spirit! You
don't want me to do this alone, so you sent me a
helper and a friend—a friend bearing gifts. I can
see my gift was chosen with me in mind; it suits me,
and it brings me joy to use it. The more aware I am
of the gifts of others, the more I seem to experience
them. Thank you for children who already show gifts
of wisdom, mercy, and discernment; they make life
so much richer! Thank you for children with gifts of
knowledge and faith, for theirs increases my own. To
recognize they are acting in the Spirit makes me feel
that much closer to you, which magnifies my joy.

What gift has God given you to minister to others?

Beloved Child

You are altogether beautiful, my love;
there is no flaw in you.
SONG OF SOLOMON 4:7 ESV

God, you make such beautiful things! I start to list them off: babies, flowers, sunsets, birds, snow—and I realize there is no end. More beautiful than anything by far are those I love. A mother's arms, a father's hands, a child's face all leave me breathless and filled with gratitude. Thank you, Lord, for such a lovely world. I know that to those who love me, I add to its beauty. This humbles me. In the mirror I see things I'd like to change: flaws, imperfections, and signs of age. Behind me, hands resting proudly on my shoulders, your eyes see your beautiful, beloved child. To you, I am more beautiful than the sunset. I am as lovely as a rose.

Do you know that God sees you as beautiful?

Sadness

Cast all your anxiety on him, because he cares for you.
1 PETER 5:7 NRSV

God, nothing makes me feel more loved by you than to know you want to carry my burdens. You would rather take on my pain than see me feel it. You prefer to bear my sadness over watching me cry. Your empathy is so great; your love is truly more than I can comprehend. I'll admit my burden grows hard to bear. Anxiety pins me down, and depression renders me unable even to try and move away. I know you see this; nothing escapes your notice. "Give it to me!" You encourage. I sometimes need your strength even to respond. Thank you, Lord, for giving it to me when I do.

What sadness can you cast on Jesus today?

Beautiful Future

"No eye has seen, no ear has heard,
and no mind has imagined
what God has prepared
for those who love him."
1 CORINTHIANS 2:9 NLT

Lord, I get anxious about the future—for myself and for my children. I try to imagine it, and it seems so vague and uncertain; all blurry around the edges. I know you know, and I know it is good—so much better than anything I am even capable of conjuring up. This beautiful future is your promise to those who love you, and oh, how I love you. Forgive my anxiety, God. I don't want to dishonor you, and I do trust you, Lord, with my life. I love that it is beyond my imagining, because what I imagine is pretty great. I'm excited to get there and see what you've done.

How do you imagine what God has prepared just for you?

A Voice

He delivers the needy when they call,
the poor and those who have no helper.
PSALM 72:12 NRSV

Father, there's someone out there with no voice, someone who has never known hope, who has no idea you exist—let alone how much you love them. Let my voice stand for his today; let my hope be hers. Infuse the helpless with a peace that makes the unendurable more than just endurable. Give them hope, God, that their situation will change. Send your angels, and send your servants, Lord, to these people I will never meet who suffer in ways I cannot imagine. Take away their hopelessness. Shine light where none has shone. Bring help where none has gone. Show them your glory!

Will you pray today for someone who has no hope, that God would reveal his love to them?

Obedience

I will keep on obeying your instructions
forever and ever.
PSALM 119:44 NLT

Father, you deserve nothing but my best. I offer you my love, my worship, my respect, but I withhold my obedience. Do the others ring hollow without it? How much do I really love you if I refuse to listen to your good advice? How can I say I respect you if I refuse to follow your instructions? Forgive me, Lord. I trust your plans for my life; I know your instructions are for my good and for your glory. You are a good Father, worthy of an obedient child. I want to obey you, Lord, so my love really looks like love and my worship comes from a place of truth. Help me to model obedience so my children feel called to do the same.

Do you want to obey God and give him your best?

My Strength

"Be strong and bold; have no fear or dread of them,
because it is the LORD your God who goes with you;
he will not fail you or forsake you."

DEUTERONOMY 31:6 NRSV

All-powerful God, because of you, I don't have to be strong. I can admit to weakness, to a lack of self-control, to fear, to whatever it is that diminishes my strength. You are strong enough for me and my family; all I have to do is believe you. You are my strength, Lord! Help me trust in this truth. Tell me—again—that I can rely on your power when mine is not enough. When I start to believe the lies that fear and temptation tell me, speak louder, and remind me you are always with me, and you never fail.

Are you relying on God to be your strength?

God Bless You

"The LORD bless you and keep you;
the LORD make his face shine on you and be gracious to you;
the LORD turn his face toward you and give you peace."
NUMBERS 6:24–26 NIV

God bless you. I say it when someone sneezes or does something thoughtful. Lord, cause me to pause. I want to speak your blessing over this person's life and extend your favor around me. Your blessings are the sweetest thing about this life; don't let me say it if I don't mean it. As I consider the true weight of those words, the joy of receiving your good gifts, I am convicted. Inspire me to sincerely, boldly, and frequently proclaim your blessing over my children's lives. Make your face shine upon them in a way that fills their hearts—and blows their minds.

Can you speak this verse over your children today?

All My Desire

Think about the things of heaven, not the things of earth.
COLOSSIANS 3:2 NLT

Beautiful Lord, when I am in your presence, everything else seems so unimportant. Material things pale in comparison to getting a fresh revelation from your Word; no amount of public approval can match feeling your pleasure; no physical pleasure comes close to the feeling of being comforted in your arms. I want all my desire to be for you, God! Give me a distaste for the things of this world and let me hunger for the things of heaven. May your will be all I seek, your offerings all I accept, and more of you all I want.

How do you think about the things of heaven instead of the things of earth?

A Giving Heart

In all things I have shown you that by working hard
in this way we must help the weak and remember
the words of the Lord Jesus, how he himself said,
"It is more blessed to give than to receive."
ACTS 20:35 ESV

Generous God, I know you love a cheerful giver, and I want to be one! I want to give joyously and to the fullest extent I can. But I can be selfish like a child with a treat or a favorite toy. I like my extras, and sometimes I listen to the voice that says I deserve them. As I cling to my luxuries, drown that voice out with your own. Remind me of how wonderful it feels to be generous. Remind me of how much I have, and how very little I need. Keep it ever before me how very many people rely on the generosity of others for those basic needs to be met. Grant me a giving heart.

Are you a cheerful giver?

It Is You

"The Helper, the Holy Spirit, whom the Father will send in My name, He will teach you all things, and bring to your remembrance all that I said to you."

JOHN 14:26 NASB

Holy Spirit, Scripture tells me you are with me. It is you who teach me, remind me, and help me through this life. It is you who responds when I call. You are both a mystery and utterly familiar. You live inside me and you surround me. You are God and you are my friend. I call you now, Spirit. Help me respond to the situation before me as Jesus would—in a way that will make my Father proud. Infuse me with your power and also your tenderness. Give me your wisdom along with your patience, and your fire along with your peace.

What do you need the Lord to remind you of for the situation you are facing?

The Same Wall

I begged the Lord three times to take
this problem away from me.
2 CORINTHIANS 12:8 NCV

Lord, you always hear me, and you always respond; your judgment is always perfect. When I'm struggling against an obstacle, remind me it could have been you who placed it there. When I keep hitting the same wall, or reaching the same dead end, let me consider that you may be encouraging me to take a new road. Forgive my stubbornness as I sometimes try to scale the barriers you put up to get my attention. I know you know best, and that you love me more than I can comprehend. Preventing me from reaching goals you haven't set for me is a sign of how dearly you care for me. Even when I don't understand it, I thank you, Father, for your perfect love.

Have you hit a wall? Does the Lord want you to take another direction?

Surrender Again

My child, give me your heart,
and let your eyes observe my ways.
PROVERBS 23:26 NRSV

I surrender, Lord. I mean it each time I offer myself to you. I trust you with my whole life and with the lives of my children. I love you with my whole heart. But sometimes I start to take it back, piece by piece. I'll just take control of my finances again. Maybe my child's future too. And yes, I think I'll just handle my physical well-being as long as I'm here. Soon enough, though, I realize I've made a mess of things. Again. So again, I surrender. Take it all, even the bits I'm trying to hide from you—to hang onto. I want to be wholly yours; only then will I be whole.

Are you taking things back that you have given to the Lord?

Compassionately

Jesus, when He came out, saw a great multitude
and was moved with compassion for them,
because they were like sheep not having a shepherd.
So He began to teach them many things.
MARK 6:34 NKJV

Father of compassion, how grateful I am for your tenderness toward me. Even when my problems are my own doing, you see me in my distress and you rescue me. Gently you restore me; I never lose my standing with you. It's incredible. You're incredible. I celebrate your compassion today, Lord. I remember the sacrifice you made because of it. You knew I could never do enough, never be enough, so you came here—as more than enough—on my behalf. Patiently you teach me, no matter how long it takes me to learn. Repeatedly you forgive me, no matter how many times I sin. Compassionately you love me. Thank you.

Have you thanked the Lord lately for his compassion toward you?

Resource of Hope

Encourage one another and build up each other,
as indeed you are doing.
1 THESSALONIANS 5:11 NRSV

God, your Word brings so much encouragement!
No matter what I am up against, there is a source of
strength, comfort, or wisdom. Because of all you've
done for me and my family, I find myself wanting to
share it—to be an encouragement to those around
me. Lord, give me a heart for the hurting; plant
Scriptures in my head that will bless them. Let me
be a resource of hope as I point others to you. Let
me be a living testimony, Father. When people see
my transformed life, let them be encouraged that it's
never too late to turn to you; you remake even the
hardest of hearts.

How can you encourage someone today?

Gratuitous Love

By grace you have been saved through faith;
and that not of yourselves, it is the gift of God;
not as a result of works, so that no one may boast.
EPHESIANS 2:8–9 NASB

Generous, loving God, of all your gifts, your grace astonishes me the most. I can never tell you enough how grateful I am for this unearned forgiveness, this gratuitous love. It must seem sometimes as if I am throwing it back in your face; forgive me for my many sins, Father. Let me remember this moment, Lord: the way it feels to ponder your unmerited favor and know that grace is mine. The fact I don't deserve it—can never deserve it—is what makes it so awesome, but don't let me use that as an excuse to stop trying. You deserve all my effort and more.

Have you pondered lately the amazing grace of God toward you?

Exercise in Hope

Be joyful because you have hope.
Be patient when trouble comes, and pray at all times.
ROMANS 12:12 NCV

God, you make everything better—even waiting. Outside your influence, I grow impatient, sometimes even second-guessing good decisions when I have to wait for an answer to prayer. Truthfully, apart from you I can barely handle a child who takes too long to do their homework, or a two-person line at the grocery store. But with you, waiting becomes an exercise in hope. Because I trust you, I can believe in the outcome of my waiting; I know it will be for my good. I am filled with hope as I await your answer, your solution, your response to my needs, my questions, my dreams. Your promise turns impatience into expectation and waiting into joy.

Are you being filled with hope as you wait for God's answer?

Compared to Glory

I consider that our present sufferings are not worth
comparing with the glory that will be revealed in us.
ROMANS 8:18 NIV

Eternal Lord, pain is so hard to endure! When I can't avoid it, and when it seems to want to linger, I need you to remind me this is not my home. The time I spend here will be just a breath in my forever with you. Tell me again that what feels like an eternity right now I won't even remember in heaven. Father, I need you to keep telling me, because pain wears me down. I start to believe I will always feel this way, and I know that's a lie. Suffering here will be reversed to joy in heaven. This momentary pain is nothing— nothing at all—compared to the joy you have for me once I am home.

Can you trust that your present pain is nothing compared to the joy that is coming?

Turn Away

No temptation has overtaken you except such as is common to man; but God is faithful, who will not allow you to be tempted beyond what you are able, but with the temptation will also make the way of escape, that you may be able to bear it.

1 CORINTHIANS 10:13 NKJV

Heavenly Father, I long to make you proud. At my best—which is when I am most connected to you—temptation is easy to resist. Compared to resting in your favor, the fleeting pleasures of sin are nothing. But I am seldom at my best. Every surrender to sin weakens that connection. Help me resist, God. Maybe if I saw it differently: not as a sign that I am weak because I am tempted, but as a sign of your strength in me because I am tempted and can turn away. Help me see temptation as a sign of your faith in me, as a chance to prove you are right to assign it.

Can you see God strengthening you as you face temptation?

Constant

This change of plans greatly upset Jonah,
and he became very angry.
JONAH 4:1 NLT

God, in a world that is always changing, it is so
wonderful to know you are just who you say and
just who you have always been. The earth and its
people constantly change, but you remain the same.
If I forget this, lift my eyes to the stars. Only you
are constant—my true north when I lose my sense
of direction. I love this about you, Lord. But I live
here, now, and I need you to help me embrace the
inconstancy of this life. Things move when I'd like
them to stay still. Remind me that you are stable.
You won't change, and you won't change your mind
about me, no matter how much I disappoint you.
Assure me that if you change my course, it's to keep
me aligned with you.

Is God changing your course? Can you trust him?

My Endurance

Since we are surrounded by so great a cloud of witnesses, let us also lay aside every weight, and sin which clings so closely, and let us run with endurance the race that is set before us.
HEBREWS 12:1 ESV

God in heaven, when I think of all who have gone before me, the "great cloud of witnesses" who cheer me on as I fight to stay this course, I know I can do it. You've empowered souls to endure the assignments you gave them since the beginning of time, and you'll be doing it long after I've joined the cloud myself. My endurance is you. It's my faith, my inspiration, my belief that heaven is watching, waiting, celebrating my run. With a cheering section like that, with a coach like you, I can't possibly fail. Thank you, Lord, for spurring me on.

How is your endurance for your race founded in God?

August

I am praying to you because I
know you will answer, O God.
Bend down and listen as I pray.

PSALM 17:6 NLT

Lead Me

"Father, if you are willing, take away this cup of suffering.
But do what you want, not what I want."
LUKE 22:42 NCV

Lord, you are perfect. Your plans are perfect. Your will for my life and the life of my children: perfect. I don't know why I cling so tightly to what I want, why it's so hard to just surrender, but it is hard. I do cling. This life is what I know; I think that is much of my struggle. I fear the unknown. I fear pain, disappointment, and failure. But you are none of those things! You are healing, joy, and victory. I know this—I know you. Please help me remember and help me surrender. Show me and lead me into your will, Father. Make it my deepest desire.

What are you clinging to that you need to surrender?

Take This Suffering

Heal me, O LORD, and I will be healed;
Save me and I will be saved,
For You are my praise.
JEREMIAH 17:14 NASB

Healer, I need you! I know what you can do; I've read it and I've seen it. Today, I claim your healing. You know my need, Father. The brokenness in body and spirit for which I pray is not news to you. You are intimately involved, waiting to intercede. I believe you, Lord. I know you can take this suffering in an instant; I know it as well as I know my name. I know that if you choose to wait, even until we are reunited, that your reasons are good. Boldly, I ask you not to wait. I ask you to act now, today, and to heal me.

Where do you need Jesus' healing touch?

With Patience

If we hope for what we do not see, we wait for it with patience.
ROMANS 8:25 NRSV

God of endless patience, you are a marvel. Not one of your children gives you the obedience you deserve, yet you never run out of kindness or second chances. My patience is so small compared to yours, yet my frustrations are incomparably less. Lord, let this truth inspire me; let it convict me. I need your patience, God, as I work to extend my own. Infuse me with supernatural tolerance, Lord! Remind me that the small offenses I react to are so very minor compared to the love I feel—and to the love I receive from you. Thank you, Lord. Let love and gratitude rule my heart.

How are you letting love and gratitude rule your heart?

Wise Enough

Blessed is the one who perseveres under trial because, having stood the test, that person will receive the crown of life that the Lord has promised to those who love him.

JAMES 1:12 NIV

Wise Lord, I don't understand this trial. I don't, but I know you do. Looking back on my life, I can see how every test, every temptation—whether I pass or fail—has shaped me, taught me, and increased my wisdom. I confess some days I feel like asking, am I wise enough yet? But of course, I know the answer, and I trust your wisdom above all. Open my heart and my lips and let me say, "Thank you, Lord! Thank you for another trial." I love learning from you, and I love learning of you. Remind me on the days I forget that tests are a chance to lean into you—then extend your arm and pull me in.

In your trials are you learning to lean on the Lord?

These Dreams

Take delight in the LORD,
and he will give you the desires of your heart.
PSALM 37:4 NRSV

Awesome God, why do I try to limit you, which limits me? I have these dreams, Father. They are big and bold they scare me, so I try to pretend they aren't there. I listen to the voice that says I'm being selfish, or the one that says it's impossible, but then I remember who you are. Can I confess something? This scares me even more. What if my wildest dream is only the beginning? Can I handle the crazy, beautiful adventure you have planned for me, this dream that won't leave my heart? Give me the courage to find out, good Father. And then—make those dreams come true.

What dreams are you waiting for God to fulfill?

As I Love

"To you who are willing to listen, I say, love your enemies!
Do good to those who hate you. Bless those who curse you.
Pray for those who hurt you."
LUKE 6:27–28 NLT

God, even you who are love itself have an enemy,
and he is mine as well. He acts through everyone
who provokes envy, self-doubt, condemnation, or
thoughts of retaliation in me. Help me respond as you
would—as you do—with open arms. As I love those
who hurt me, I take away the power of the enemy.
I make them a friend. If they don't love me back, so
much the better. It gives me more to pray for, which
in turn draws me closer to you. I bless those who
have hurt me and ask you to touch their lives with
your loving kindness.

**Is there someone who has hurt you that needs Jesus
to touch their life?**

No Reason

God has not given us a spirit of fear,
but of power and of love and of a sound mind.
2 TIMOTHY 1:7 NKJV

God, you are my protector, my comforter, my strength, and my salvation. I have no reason to fear. And yet, I fear. I expect you spoke of our fear so often because you knew it would be one of our biggest strangleholds. I confess it's cutting off my breath even as I pray. Forgive me for my fear, Lord. Help me to see it as a sin against you, who have proven time and again I can depend on you. I know you are stronger than all my fear; you are stronger even than death. Remind me, remind me, and remind me again. Give me your power, your love, and a sound mind. You are my strength. I have no reason to fear.

Do you believe that God is stronger than your fear?

Help Me

"The LORD will fight for you, and you have only to be silent."
EXODUS 14:14 ESV

Lord, I need help! So much, I don't even know where to begin, what to ask for. Life has me overwhelmed as I try to work and live and love inside your will. Thank you, Father, that I don't have to know where to begin. You are my champion. You know exactly what I need, and exactly when and how to deliver me. Help me to stop my thrashing, my shouting, my struggling against this weight and just be still. Only when I sit calmly before you—and bring the entire burden with me—can you answer my call for help. Only then will I hear your response; only then can you lift us both—me and my burden—and take over the fight.

Are you able to be silent and let God fight for you?

Unshakable

> "The steadfast of mind You will keep in perfect peace,
> Because he trusts in You."
> ISAIAH 8:9 NASB

God who sees and hears and knows everything, how is it you have perfect peace? I can't comprehend it. Within minutes of waking, the enemies of my peace are jabbing away at me. The weight of responsibility, memories of disappointment, and a vague sense of dread sometimes greet me before my feet hit the floor. Greet them back, Father, with your peace. Bless me with your sight, so that responsibilities become privileges, memories are wisdom gained, and dread is replaced with joyful anticipation. Make me unshakable, God. This world will come at me until the day I die, but I don't have to let it catch me. Instead, I will pursue and claim your peace.

How can you trust God to calm you and give you his peace?

Growing Wiser

The wisdom that comes from God is first of all pure, then peaceful, gentle, and easy to please. This wisdom is always ready to help those who are troubled and to do good for others. It is always fair and honest.

JAMES 3:17 NCV

Wise Father, help me to know when I am following you and when I have wandered off on my own. When I do stray—and we both know I will—let me learn and grow wiser. Use my mistakes, my stumbles into pride or selfish ambition or unearned rest to reinforce my love of the road you've chosen. Your way is perfect; if opposition, unrest, and compromise rise up to meet me, remind me these things are not from you. When the way is lovely, when my heart is full, let me revel in your company. I know you are there!

Where do you need God's wisdom today?

Enough Today

In all circumstances take up the shield of faith, with which you can extinguish all the flaming darts of the evil one.
EPHESIANS 6:16 ESV

Faithful God, you are always for me. When my circumstances cause me to doubt your steadfastness and question your plan, increase my faith! As I struggle against where you've placed me, add to my faith again. Help me accept what I did not ask for through this conviction: you are faithful, and my faith is in you. Though you already know it, I'll confess it: I don't always want this situation. This constant sacrifice. I'm struggling to accept it. Can it be enough today that I accept you? Will you build on that until I stop resisting and settle in? Remind me you are here, Father. In knowing that, let me see that here is where I'm meant to be.

Have you taken up the shield of faith to help you resist the evil one?

Burning Joy

"Go your way, eat the fat and drink sweet wine and send portions of them to those for whom nothing is prepared, for this day is holy to our LORD; and do not be grieved, for the joy of the LORD is your strength."

NEHEMIAH 8:10 NRSV

Lord, you are so good to me. Even on the darkest day, your joy burns inside me. That flame gives me strength when mine is gone. It allows me to rejoice with those who rejoice, even though I mourn. It allows me to give and to serve, even though I need. It gives me life, Father. How I thank you for that! I don't really understand it. How can I smile when there is no reason? How can I carry this load, though all my strength is depleted? I don't understand it, but I know your ways are higher than mine. Fan the flame, Lord. Let your joy consume me, replacing all that would break me down.

Wouldn't you love the joy of the Lord to consume you?

Everything

"You will seek me and find me
when you seek me with all your heart."
JEREMIAH 29:13 NIV

Wonderful God, as I consider the next chapter of my life, as I dream and plan for a future only you can know, remind me of the one thing I need. No matter what the future holds for me and my children, your plan is perfect. Your love is unfailing. Everything I'm looking for is in you. Take my whole heart, Lord, and make our future certain. When I seek answers, point me to you. When I seek direction, lead me to you. When I seek purpose, steer me to you. Remind me that all I'm after, every answer I yearn for, is contained in you.

How are you seeking Jesus with all your heart?

Humble Servant

"If anyone slaps you on one cheek, offer him
the other cheek, too. If someone takes your coat,
do not stop him from taking your shirt."
LUKE 6:29 NCV

Father God, in the image of Jesus make me your
humble servant. Call to mind his willingness to suffer
for those who would harm him, his kindness toward
the unkind, his relentless love of the unlovable. It's so
much easier to serve those I deem "worthy," Lord.
Give me your eyes so I can see the worthiness of all.
Break my heart for those who would break mine. Let
me see the pain that causes them to behave as they
do and let the seeing move me. Let me forget myself,
God! Allow my thoughts of me to diminish, and my
heart for the broken to overflow.

Has God given you a heart for the brokenhearted?

Distant Meaning

You are a chosen generation, a royal priesthood, a holy nation,
His own special people, that you may proclaim the praises of
Him who called you out of darkness into His marvelous light.
1 PETER 2:9 NKJV

Lord, everything you do is on purpose, and all you
allow has purpose. As I seek your grand intention
for my life, help me to remember there is meaning in
the here and now—in the chores, and tasks, and
monotonous daily schedules. Whatever dark corner
I find myself in, you have called me to shine your
light. Pull my focus out, Father. The darkness is
everywhere, but it diminishes the moment I cast your
reflection. Keep my eyes on the light, especially when
purpose and meaning seem distant. Bring value to my
waiting by letting me bring light to the room in which
I wait.

**Does purpose and meaning for your life seem distant?
Ask God to reveal the value of waiting today.**

Equal Trust

So be strong and courageous,
all you who put your hope in the LORD!
PSALM 31:24 NLT

Precious Lord, your trustworthiness is unmatched.
You cannot lie. You are love itself. How can I possibly
question you? What room does fear presume to
claim in my heart? Yet here it is. Here I am asking:
yes, I know he can, but will he? Will you increase my
trust? Remind me you are not of this world, which
fails me time and again. Remind me of your unfailing
love and of how deeply I love you. I want to trust you
as much as I love you, Lord! I want to trust you as
much as you love me: unlimited, unending, to the ends
of the earth.

Can you trust the Lord as much as you love him?

With Help

I will instruct you and teach you the way you should go;
I will counsel you with my eye upon you.
PSALM 32:8 NRSV

God, you are the perfect teacher, the ideal boss, the ultimate parent. I am none of these, and I'm feeling the weight of that. You've given me responsibility for another person, Lord, and I don't always feel up to the task. Lead me, teach me, love me through my failures. I have so many shortcomings. How can I be an influence? I'm in such need of grace. How can I give it away? With your help. With your help, I can do anything. I can love the most unlovable behavior, forgive the most unforgivable offense, and accept the most unacceptable circumstances. Even as I pray it, I feel the weight. With your help, Lord. Only with your help.

How are you letting the Lord instruct and teach you in the way you should go?

Hope Wins

We also have joy with our troubles, because we know that these troubles produce patience. And patience produces character, and character produces hope.

ROMANS 5:3–4 NCV

Lord, can I confess something to you? Some days, I wish you didn't have so much faith in me. I wish I were ordinary—less than ordinary, even—and that you were finished building my character. Some days, this life is just a little too much. Other days, I wouldn't trade this crazy, complicated roller-coaster ride for anything this side of eternity. I see the incredible blessing this suffering brings, and I revel in the intimacy of a life lived utterly dependent on you. My troubles bring me joy as I feel my patience growing. My patience makes me stronger. It's still hard—so very hard—but I know that hope will win.

How do you see your troubles producing joy, patience, character, and hope?

Rest Awhile

All who have entered into God's rest have rested from their
labors, just as God did after creating the world.
HEBREWS 4:10 NLT

Lord, I'm tired. I'm racing toward some things as
I run from others; I'm climbing a hill while dodging
boulders as they fall. I need a respite: from the things
the world heaves toward me and from the things I
pull upon myself. Some days I'm not even sure which
is which. I am coming to rest awhile with you. You
give supernatural strength—in body and in soul—
and that is exactly what I need. Draw me into your
peace, God. Under your protection, even if I can't
stop all my labor, I know I'll find relief.

**Are you tired? Do you need to stop and find rest in
your heavenly Father?**

If I Quit

If we endure, we will also reign with Him;
if we deny Him, He also will deny us.
2 TIMOTHY 2:12 NASB

Lord, your love endures forever. Your patience knows no end. Your mercies are constantly renewed. You never stop, God! It's yet another mystery I cannot grasp. My patience runs out; my mercy has limits; even my love can be capricious. When things are hard, I want to give up. Remind me, God, why it matters that I keep going. Impress upon me that the only way to be with the one who never stops is to never stop! If I quit, this is where I'll stay. If I persevere, I'll make it to the end. If I make it to the end, I'll be there with you.

Are you ready to quit, or can you endure to the end with God's help?

Let Go

A time to seek, and a time to lose;
a time to keep, and a time to cast away.
ECCLESIASTES 3:6 NRSV

God, everything on heaven and earth is yours. This includes me, and everything and everyone you've entrusted to my care. I grow attached, start to see things as mine. Especially those you gave me to love, Lord! I love them so, and that love has given me purpose. And now it's time for something new, for both of us. Help me let go, Father! Help me move into the next season of loving them, the next season of purpose for my life. I know it's time. Pry my arms from around them and open them up to you. Help me return what was always yours, and to welcome what comes next.

Are you ready to let go and welcome what God has next for you?

My Comforter

"Take my yoke upon you. Let me teach you,
because I am humble and gentle at heart,
and you will find rest for your souls."
MATTHEW 11:29 NLT

Jesus, just to say your name quiets my racing heart. To remember all you are and all you have done brings comfort to my soul. I need that today, Lord. Your presence, your gentleness, your quiet example of a life at peace: the comfort of your love restores my hope. How can I begin to thank you for the relief you bring? What can I give you? You are my comforter, Jesus. Your selfless hands wipe away every anxious tear. Your strong arms lift my burdens, replacing them with the easy task of loving you in return.

What burden are you carrying that you need to give to Jesus?

Your Faithfulness

My covenant I will not break,
Nor alter the word that has gone out of My lips.
PSALM 89:34 NKJV

Lord, you are so faithful! Never have you broken a promise; every commitment is honored. I wish I could say the same. Each time I break my word, I feel like I've dishonored you as well. I want to reflect your faithfulness, God—to be utterly reliable. Selfishness tells me it's okay to go back on a promise; laziness says I deserve a break from my striving. Drown them out, Father, with reminders of your steadfast loyalty. Make me in your image: faithful and true. Convict me with a desire to honor every commitment in your name. Create a heart of integrity and reliability in me so my word is golden.

Do you know that the Lord can help you keep true to your word?

Some of Heaven

How abundant are the good things
that you have stored up for those who fear you,
that you bestow in the sight of all,
on those who take refuge in you.

PSALM 31:19 NIV

Wonderful God, most of what I know of your goodness I've learned from people who love you. The selflessness of a heart surrendered to you is the most beautiful thing I've ever seen, and only a glimpse of the ways you are good. This blows me away: how can you contain it all? And what more could there possibly be? Generosity, humility, sacrifice, wisdom, patience. These are things your children bring to light and I am so grateful! It inspires me to be more like you, this unconditional love from my children and friends. Thank you for bringing some of heaven to earth through them.

Who are some of the people that have shown you God's goodness and love?

Protect My Heart

Do not be fooled: "Bad friends will ruin good habits."
1 CORINTHIANS 15:33 NCV

Lord, your influence leads to life. Only goodness is in you, and it is all I want in me. I sometimes feel like the more I desire to be good, the more the enemy tempts me to do bad. He brings people into my life who tell me a little gossip never hurt anyone, or a little indulgence is no big deal. Protect my heart, God, from anyone who would persuade me to go against your will. Make me sensitive to the people around whom I'm tempted to compromise; help me see they are not on my side. Surround me with those who reflect you, so I will do the same.

Do you have any friends that God is asking you to run away from?

Paved Road

Without consultation, plans are frustrated,
But with many counselors they succeed.
PROVERBS 15:22 NASB

Lord, you are the wise counselor. You know the path we all should take because it's the one you yourself designed. I want to give good advice, God, especially when these children I love are making plans for their lives. I want to send them down the road you paved, not the one the enemy has designed to distract them. Attune me to your will, Lord. Plant your wisdom in me. Give me an ear for truth, and an eye for spotting any deviation from it. Inspire their dreams and inspire my counsel, aligning both to your perfect plan. Protect them as they go and reward their plans with success.

Who has God put in your life to counsel? Are you leading them to him?

Words of Life

"I tell you, on the day of judgment you will have to give an account for every careless word you utter; for by your words you will be justified, and by your words you will be condemned."
MATTHEW 12:36–37 NRSV

Lord, your words are beautiful, life giving, and inspiring. I wish all of mine were the same. When I think of how many times I've said something and then wished I could take it back—or worse, the times I wasn't even sorry for the hurtful things I uttered—I know I need your forgiveness. And what of the careless words, the ones that didn't even register to me, but have done damage I can't repair? You can do the impossible, and I pray you will. Mend the hearts I've hurt with my words, including mine and my children's. When unkindness or criticism tries to leave my mouth, let it be caught in my throat. Then fill me with words that give life, and a desire to share those words with others.

Are you careful to speak only words that give life?

It Makes Sense

He heals the brokenhearted
and bandages their wounds.
PSALM 147:3 NLT

Lord, my healer, come close and mend my brokenness. I'm fragile, and my wounds have left me a little bit afraid, even of you. I can't help but question how you could allow me to hurt this much. I still have enough faith to cry out to you, but just about everything else has been stripped away. God, thank you for allowing this honesty. I know you are good, and I know that even this will make sense to me one day, but today I hurt, and I ache, and I don't understand at all—and it's okay with you for me to say so. Just this awareness begins my healing. Come closer, God, and mend me further.

If you are hurting and aching do you know that God can bring healing?

Wise Words

Do not believe every spirit, but test the spirits,
whether they are of God; because many
false prophets have gone out into the world.
1 JOHN 4:1 NKJV

God, nothing compares to the thrill of hearing from you. I long to encounter your Spirit, and the moments I feel your hand on my life are as good as it gets. I know there are those who would take advantage of my openness; yours is not the only spirit at work in this world. So, grant me discernment, Lord, and give me an ear for truth. Remind me not to seek the thrill of the supernatural, but the thrill of encountering you. Especially when someone tells me exactly what I want to hear, have me question if it is something you would say. Make me wise to your words, God, and turn me away from all competing voices.

Do you test what you hear to make sure it is from God?

For the Good

We know that in all things God works for the good of those who love him, who have been called according to his purpose.

ROMANS 8:28 NIV

God, even when I've lost hope in my circumstances and have no faith in my situation, thank you that I can always trust your purpose. Even when things turn tragic, you find a way to give birth to beauty. I know I doubt this sometimes and wallow in the pain of the moment. Thank you for not leaving me there. Lord, I need you to remind me again that your purpose will prevail. I believe it; I know it; but I need to feel it today as well. Just a glimpse of the good that's coming, a peek at future beauty is all I need, and my hope will be restored.

Do you believe that God is working all things together for your good?

My Intercessor

In the same way the Spirit also helps our weakness;
for we do not know how to pray as we should,
but the Spirit Himself intercedes for us
with groanings too deep for words.
ROMANS 8:26 NASB

Lord, how I thank you for your Holy Spirit! The friendship, assistance, power, and gifts would each be enough on their own, but he brings them all together. And then, on the days I am too lost or broken to even call out to you for help, he becomes my intercessor. When I don't know what to say, when only whimpers and moans come forth, he translates on my behalf, making you aware of just how to heal me. How deeply you love us, Lord, to give us such an intimate friend! And once I grasp this, how increased is my love for you.

Do you realize how deeply God loves you and that he wants to be your intimate friend?

September

"Keep watch and pray,
so that you will not give in to
temptation. For the spirit is
willing, but the body is weak!"

MATTHEW 26:41 NLT

Hope in the Light

"Behold, I am doing a new thing;mnow it springs forth,
do you not perceive it? I will make a way in
the wilderness and rivers in the desert."
ISAIAH 43:19 ESV

God, I thank you that you are the God of renewal. The sunset and sunrise remind me of your constant invention, your continual refreshment of my life. My head may hit the pillow in frustration and grief, but with the morning my eyes open to possibility and the first steps of healing. What feels like despair in the dark shows itself as hope in the light. Thank you, God, for newness. Thank you for forgiveness and a clean slate, for mercies that renew at dawn. And thank you most of all for the newness in me. With every waking my faith is strengthened, and my hope renewed. Help me to reflect this hope in the morning so my children also feel renewed as they awaken each day.

Can you perceive that God is doing a new thing in you?

Brave Enough

Lying lips are an abomination to the LORD,
but those who act faithfully are his delight.
PROVERBS 12:22 NRSV

Lord, there is no deceit in you. You never try to trick me or mislead me, and your only true enemy is called the father of lies. So why, when I claim to follow you, do I lie? I hate lies, from my mouth or the mouths of my children. I want us to experience the joy of transparency before you. Help us not to justify it: the truth might hurt them; the truth might hurt me; the truth isn't interesting enough, so we embellish— just a little. Harmless. Except it isn't. It harms our reputation, both here and with you. It hurts you, and that hurts me. Forgive our lies, Father, and make us brave enough to tell the truth. Even when it might hurt, remind us lies hurt worse.

Are you brave enough to tell the truth?

Great Things

Using the Scriptures, the person who serves God will be capable, having all that is needed to do every good work.
2 TIMOTHY 3:17 NCV

God, I know you don't need us, but I pray you will use us. We want to achieve great things in your name, whether it's to just a handful of people or to thousands or even millions. I'm so grateful for what you've done in my family's lives, and I'm so excited about the purpose you gave each of us. I want to serve you and bring you glory. Please equip me, Lord. Plant your Word in my heart and empower me with the ability to reflect your goodness. No matter how large or how small the assignment, let my life be of service, and may it bring you the glory you deserve.

How do you want God to use you?

The Right Path

A man's heart plans his way,
But the LORD directs his steps.
PROVERBS 16:9 NKJV

God, I had it all planned out. I prayed for your blessing and set off on my way. Only I didn't get my way. Things didn't turn out like I hoped; where I ended up is not what I planned. Does this mean you didn't answer, or could it be that you did? I know you know best, Father, so if I ask for your blessing and you don't respond as I'm hoping, I have to believe that is the blessing. It's hard to remember this in my disappointment, and I may even have doubted your attentiveness to me. Thank you for forgiving me, Lord, and for putting me on the right path—whether I asked you to or not.

Do you feel like you are on God's path for your life?

One Thing

"God so loved the world that he gave his
one and only Son, that whoever believes in him
shall not perish but have eternal life."
JOHN 3:16 NIV

God, may I never lose my wonder at the beautiful truth of John 3:16. May I forever be astonished that you would sacrifice your perfect Son, your deeply beloved, for me. I think of the little ones I love most in this world—of how badly it hurts to see them suffer even slightly—and the magnitude of Jesus' sacrifice and the depth of your love overwhelm me. You've made it so easy, Father. Just one thing you ask of me: believe. How can that be the only price? It's too good; you're too good! And how can I keep this to myself? I cannot. I will not. Praise you, Lord, for all you've done.

Isn't it wonderful that Jesus died to give you eternal life?

Only Home

Do not neglect to show hospitality to strangers,
for thereby some have entertained angels unawares.
HEBREWS 13:2 ESV

Lord, you are the ultimate host, preparing everyone who comes to you a room in your home. There are no strangers, no beggars, no margins where you are: there is only home. Oh God, I fall so short in my imitation of you in this regard! I open my home when it's convenient and clean. I open my heart under pretty much the same circumstances. What opportunities have I missed, Lord? What angels have you sent for me to entertain, only to have me rush past them without a thought? Increase my hospitality, Father, in my home and in my heart, that I might bless and be blessed in return. Send your angels, Lord, and let me welcome them home.

Wouldn't it be great to find out that you had entertained angels with your hospitality?

Only Love

Love each other with genuine affection,
and take delight in honoring each other.
ROMANS 12:10 NLT

Oh Lord, every day it seems a new prejudice
pops up, or an old one is acted out with violence
and disregard for the wonderful, myriad ways you
created us. I can only imagine how your heart aches
when one of your children tears another person
down. You love them both, and you call me to do the
same. There are none who have gone too far to earn
your forgiveness; if there were, what hope would
there be for me? Imprint this on my heart. There
are no politics in heaven; there is only love. Help me
remember this. There is no hatred in heaven, only
love. Never let me forget.

**Do you love others with genuine affection and take
delight in honoring them?**

More Like You

I am sure of this, that he who began a good work in you
will bring it to completion at the day of Jesus Christ.
PHILIPPIANS 1:6 ESV

Lord, author and finisher of my faith, be the author
and finisher of my life. I'm so glad you finish all that
you start, because although I see changes, I long
to be transformed by the power of your love in me.
Each time I find myself responding in a new way, a
way that is more like you, Jesus, I rejoice. Conform
me to your image, Lord, until my transformation
is complete. Don't stop reworking my heart until
every trace of hardness and every selfish thought
are gone. Keep replacing my thoughts until only love
remains. I want to be unrecognizable except as a
reflection of you to my children and to others I
meet today.

Are you longing to be transformed by Jesus?

Adversity

"My grace is sufficient for you, for power is perfected in weakness." Most gladly, therefore, I will rather boast about my weaknesses, so that the power of Christ may dwell in me.
2 CORINTHIANS 12:9 NASB

God, I love how you turn things upside down in your kingdom. To see weakness as strength and adversity as a blessing is a concept I could not fathom were it not for your work in my life. Even now, there are days I don't see it, whether through stubbornness or lack of insight I cannot say. What I can say is that I've felt it. When I am at my weakest, I feel your strength surge through me, enabling me to fight well past my own endurance. It is at my emptiest that you come and fill me. When I'm at my lowest, I feel your grace lift me up, allowing others to see its saving power. I want my children to understand your grace as well. Show me the best way I can do that for them.

Do you need God's strength to surge through you today?

Love Never Ends

A thousand years in your sight
are like a day that has just gone by,
or like a watch in the night.
PSALM 90:4 NIV

Lord, to comprehend all you have seen, all you have heard, all you have done—and that you remember it all—is too much. Your wisdom is infinite. Your love is eternal. I've watched the children in my life grow and change, and I say I've loved them "forever," but you watch and love all of humanity all our lives. That's forever. When I realize I'll be there with you—where love never ends and where there is no time—I'm filled with wonder. I get to spend eternity with you; you designed it that way. I was made for you, and so eternity was made for me! It's so beautiful, Lord, so exciting. I can't wait to be with you and love you forever.

Are you filled with wonder knowing that you will spend an eternity with Jesus?

The Same Hands

"You have also given me the shield of Your salvation;
your gentleness has made me great."
2 SAMUEL 22:36 NKJV

Mighty God, filled with unstoppable power, your gentleness toward your children is amazing. With a breath you could annihilate us, yet you use your breath to carry words of love and the promise of healing. You never lose patience with us, giving us every opportunity to right our wrongs and come to you. Thank you, Lord, for being so tender with me. The hands that built the earth and could tear it down just as easily are the same hands that hold me when I am afraid or sad or hurting. The voice that spoke a universe into being is the same voice that whispers in my ear, I love you, my darling child. I am with you, always.

Isn't it awesome that your mighty God whispers in your ear that he loves you?

No Words

They sat on the ground with him for seven days
and seven nights. No one said a word to him,
because they saw how great his suffering was.
JOB 2:13 NIV

Lord, it's so easy to praise you and be grateful when you give to us—so easy to know what to say to someone who is celebrating. But in times of loss, the words don't come as easily. I want to be a comfort and to share your love, but how do I speak when there are no words? Please remind me that being there for someone doesn't always mean talking them through their pain. I don't need words that explain, justify, or minimize their loss; I need arms that encircle them and a heart that breaks with theirs. Help me comfort as you would, Lord: wordlessly and filled with love.

Is there someone that needs you to just sit with them and love them?

When Glory Comes

We thank God! He gives us the victory
through our Lord Jesus Christ.
1 CORINTHIANS 15:57 NCV

God, you will always be victorious. Regardless of how things appear to my eyes, you are winning. Love is winning. Each time I claim a victory, I have you to thank. May I never forget that! If I succeed, it's because you will it. If I fail, it is part of your plan. You are preparing me for victories to come. But it is always you, never just me. Protect my heart as I succeed, Lord. Give me the spoils of victory in Christ: gratitude, humility, and praise. When glory comes my way, let my face be a reflector straight to heaven. Yours is the victory, and to you be all the glory.

When was the last time you thanked God for victory in your life?

Bring Them Near

Bear one another's burdens,
and thereby fulfill the law of Christ.
GALATIANS 6:2 NASB

Father, from the beginning you intended relationship. We are meant to do life together—and with you. You desire intimacy with us, and you inspire it between us. But I get so isolated, Lord. Sometimes of my own doing: I retreat inward, focusing on my home, family, and responsibilities, nurturing my own hurts and pretending it's enough. Other times, I'm simply left out or forgotten. Neither is what you intended. I am meant to bear the burdens of others, and they are meant to bear mine. Bring them near, and then strengthen me enough to let them in so we can fulfill your law of love.

Do you have someone that helps you bear your burdens?

You Are Abba

Whoever spares the rod hates his son,
but he who loves him is diligent to discipline him.
PROVERBS 13:24 ESV

Father, just as I never imagined thanking my earthly parents for disciplining me, I never saw myself coming to you in gratitude for your discipline. I like thinking of you as Abba, Daddy, just cuddling me up and doling out blessings. But you are also Father, and like any good father, you sometimes need to administer correction. Thank you, Lord, for the timeouts, the restrictions, the times you said no. You are making me better, safer, and stronger. Just as I would never allow my children to do or have anything they wanted, so you withhold from me what will not do me good. Because you love me, you will always do me good.

Have you ever thanked the Lord for disciplining you?

Access to Wisdom

"Call to me and I will answer you, and will tell you great and hidden things that you have not known."
JEREMIAH 33:3 NRSV

Wise Lord, you contain all the knowledge and understanding there is and will ever be. And as your child, I have access to your wisdom. I'm invited to listen to you, to study your movements, to stand in your presence. How awesome. And how baffling that I so often fail to avail myself of this incredible blessing. I rely on the ideas of mortals, or worse, my own. Don't give up on me, God. Keep reminding me your wisdom is mine for the asking, that you have every answer and you invented every solution. Please keep calling to me. I want to know your great and hidden things.

Has the Lord shown you any great and hidden things?

You Alone

No one is holy like the LORD!
There is no one besides you;
there is no Rock like our God.
1 SAMUEL 2:2 NLT

Holy, holy, holy God, there is no one like you.
Nothing and no one else worthy of the word. You are
perfect, complete, pure. Forgive me for how loosely
I throw around the words that describe you, as if
anything here could compare. You are awesome;
a delicious meal is merely a delicious meal. You are
incredible; a gifted musician is simply that. You are
invincible; our government and our defenses are
under your protection. But you—you alone—
are holy.

Have you taken time to ponder God's holiness?

Every Chance

> "I am the way, the truth, and the life.
> No one comes to the Father except through Me."
> JOHN 14:6 NKJV

Lord, Father of opportunity, every good thing in my life is from you. I pray for the wisdom to recognize those good things and the courage to run from opportunities that are attractive but will ultimately lead me away from the life you've chosen for me. Every chance worth taking is a chance you gave me; every successful result ordained by you before my birth. Forgive me for leaping at everything shiny before discerning if the opportunity was divinely orchestrated. Remind me to ask myself, will this draw me closer to God? Is this in line with my purpose? And when the answer is no, strengthen me to leave it behind. You are the way I choose to follow. I know your way will be most beneficial for myself and my children.

Have you taken any chances with God lately?

Delight in Weakness

That is why, for Christ's sake, I delight in weaknesses,
in insults, in hardships, in persecutions, in difficulties.
For when I am weak, then I am strong.
2 CORINTHIANS 12:10 NIV

Wonderful God, when I am at my worst, you are at your best. The lower I get, the higher you raise me—when I remember to take your hand. Thank you, Lord, for never withdrawing it. As long as it takes and as low as I sink, you are there with your infinite strength to pull me from my weakness. You don't let me get too comfortable down here, especially when I start to think of the bottom of this pit as my home. If it's a pit of sin, you offer forgiveness; if it's sickness, you offer healing; if it's persecution and hardship, you offer rescue. You are so faithful, God! I give you all the glory.

Do you need God to rescue you from something?

All Honor

The answer is, if you eat or drink, or if you do anything,
do it all for the glory of God.

1 CORINTHIANS 10:31 NCV

God, how do you keep track of us all, our busy comings and goings? I can scarcely keep track of my own schedule. In all honesty, sometimes I cannot. I take on more than I should because I like to be busy, especially when I am working to honor you. To keep the honesty going, I also enjoy the recognition of others when I am able to keep so many balls in the air. And then I drop one. As it falls to the ground and I scramble to keep the others aloft, I have to ask, am I honoring you in that moment, or am I honoring myself? Let the answer always be you, Lord. And let all my work glorify you.

Is your work honoring God or yourself?

Just Us

The faith which you have, have as your own conviction before God. Happy is he who does not condemn himself in what he approves.

ROMANS 14:22 NASB

Precious, sinless Lord, the day you showed me the depth of my sin and my need of your salvation was the most uncomplicated day of my life. It was just us, you and I, as you made me aware of my sins and convinced me of your utter forgiveness. Then the world stepped in. Everyone has an opinion, Lord. But I don't want to be convicted by the world—by the church, by those who have read more and lived more, by even my most trusted friends. I want to be convicted by you, as before, in my own heart. Remind me again of my total faith in you, my total dependence on you, and the things I need to leave at your feet.

Do you have total faith and dependence in God?

Powerful Presence

You make known to me the path of life;
in your presence there is fullness of joy;
at your right hand are pleasures forevermore.
PSALM 16:11 ESV

Beautiful God, you are here. Even when I can't feel you, you are here. Thank you, Lord, for your powerful presence. I live for the times I can sense your Spirit, when I feel your love surrounding me and your power running through me. That's when I feel most alive, and I experience such joy. How is it that you have deemed me worthy to be so near you? What can I ever do to actually deserve such an honor? Thank you, thank you, Lord for your nearness. You don't leave me, no matter what I do or say. Your joy is always before me. Please, God, let me experience it today.

How are you experiencing God's fullness of joy in your life?

Life of Integrity

For our sake he made him to be sin who knew no sin,
so that in him we might become the righteousness of God.
2 CORINTHIANS 5:21 NRSV

Lord Jesus, thank you for showing me what it means to live of a life of integrity. In every situation, I can look to you for a model of how to live whole. What I see in your example is peace instead of panic, forgiveness instead of condemnation, and love instead of hatred. In every interaction, I see that love. Lord, you keep your promises. Your patience is an endless spring. Your faith and your faithfulness are unwavering. You are perfect, complete, whole. These are the things I will pursue if only to demonstrate to my children the importance of integrity before you.

How can you pursue the righteousness of God?

What I Would Do

"If the world hates you, remember that it hated me first."
JOHN 15:18 NLT

Oh God, every time I think of the persecution Jesus faced, I just don't understand it. How could a message so beautiful and pure—a message of love and forgiveness for everyone—be met with such hatred and fear? Lord, how would I have responded to you had I met you face-to-face? Would I have loved and pursued you, or would I have been swept up in the groundswell of fear and suspicion? I want to believe I'd have followed you right up onto the cross, but as I say that from a position of safety, freedom, and comfort, I can only pray that it's true. Jesus, make me the fearless follower I long to be!

Is Jesus making you a fearless follower of him?

Greater Impact

Commit your work to the LORD,
and your plans will be established.
PROVERBS 16:3 NKJV

Lord, everything you do matters. You've never made an idle move or thoughtless decision in all of eternity. I usually accomplish both those things before my children start school. Lord, I want to be as intentional, focused, and dedicated to the assignments you've given me as you are to me. Help me, God, as I strive to make every day matter. As I prove my trustworthiness, I pray you will give me more and more meaningful assignments with greater and greater impact. As I plan, I pray you will inspire me to consider my purpose in your kingdom. And when I slip into carelessness, I pray you will gently guide me back into intentionality.

Are you intentional, focused, and dedicated?

The Source

All praise to God, the Father of our Lord Jesus Christ.
God is our merciful Father and the source of all comfort.
2 CORINTHIANS 1:3 NLT

God, you are the source of all comfort. When I find comfort in the advice of my mother, it's because you give her the tenderness and the words. When I run to the arms of my father, you gave him the gentleness and strength to hold me just right. When I am consoled by the compassion of a friend, it is you who soften their heart toward me. Lord, forgive me for looking straight to the world, even the loved ones you gave me. Help me remember to start with you— the source—and to let you guide me from there. I often find when I do this, I need not go any further. Sometimes, just to seek and find you is all I need.

Do you go to Jesus as your source of comfort?

Anchored

Let him ask in faith, with no doubting, for he who doubts
is like a wave of the sea driven and tossed by the wind.
JAMES 1:6 NKJV

God, your Word is filled with proof of your
faithfulness and capability. Nowhere is there an
instance of you dropping the ball. My future is
secure. I am certain, yet I doubt. I believe, yet I am
skeptical. Like a ball in the ocean, I bounce around
from one wave to the next. I feel at the mercy of
wind and waves. I don't know what will take away
my questions; that's why I am calling on you.
When I ask you for something, let me ask with the
confidence of someone who already knows the
answer. Help me with my doubt, Father! Take it
away; replace it with trust. I want to be anchored,
steady and sure.

**Are you being driven and tossed by the wind?
Have you found your anchor in Jesus?**

Meet Me

It is not yet time for the message to come true,
but that time is coming soon; the message will come true.
It may seem like a long time, but be patient and wait for it,
because it will surely come; it will not be delayed.
HABAKKUK 3:2 NCV

God, you know the right time for everything. I tend to doubt this when your timing clashes with my desires, but later, when your timing is revealed, I see without fail that it is better. Sometimes it's dramatic: a missed traffic light saves me and my children from an accident. A missed opportunity leads to a far better one. Other times, you are more subtle. I love this. Since I have to wait, I slow down and watch—trying to discern what you are up to. And I do see things, like beauty and humor, that I certainly would have missed. Thank you for slowing me down, Lord, and for making me wait. Not only is your timing better, but you meet me in the waiting bearing beauty and peace.

Isn't it hard sometimes to wait for God's timing?

Staying Focused

Love is patient, love is kind. It does not envy,
it does not boast, it is not proud.
1 CORINTHIANS 13:4 NIV

Father, thank you for my life. I love our closeness.
I love you. I regret the time I spend comparing it
to the lives of others, thinking that a newer house,
a more talented child, a more prominent position,
or any host of other things would make me more
fulfilled. Your love makes me fulfilled. I know this is
true. Even to be jealous of others' intimacy with you
dishonors you, and I am sorry for it, God. The time
and attention you give them takes not one second
away from intimacy available to me. I know this
too. Help me keep my focus here, Father, on the
satisfaction of living in your love.

Are you satisfied with living in the Father's love?

Reconciliation

"My people who are called by My name
humble themselves and pray and seek My face and
turn from their wicked ways, then I will hear from heaven,
will forgive their sin and will heal their land."
2 CHRONICLES 7:14 NASB

Lord, I love to meet with you, to sing to you, to serve alongside others who are called to love you. I love to bring my sins before you and lay them at your feet, to reconcile—along with others—my heart with yours. I know repentance matters to you, God. You speak of it so often in your Word, so I pray today for churches. I hope we are getting it right and keeping the focus on love and repentance and growing intimately with you. I pray we are not making our places of reconciliation into places of entertainment. I pray we remember, before we celebrate and serve and sing, to reconcile ourselves to you.

How can you live a life of humility before the Lord?

October

Answer me when I pray to you,
my God who does what is right.
Make things easier for me when I am in trouble.
Have mercy on me and hear my prayer.

PSALM 4:1 NCV

Guard My Heart

Set your minds on things that are above,
not on things that are on earth.

COLOSSIANS 3:2 NASB

God, I love your creation! This world is dazzling in its beauty, opportunity, and variety. It's also a huge distraction, and one I am very susceptible to. Please guard my heart from worldliness, Father! I want to appreciate and respect the work of your hands without it turning to worship. Lift my eyes heavenward when they stray too long on my possessions or my body, God! Help me to be grateful for my home without turning it into an idol. Help me dedicate myself to motherhood without allowing it to consume me. Help me respect and care for my body without feeling like it defines me. Only you define me, and I want your love to be all that consumes me.

Have you set your mind on the things that are above?

This Is Temporary

We do not look at the things which are seen, but at the things which are not seen. For the things which are seen are temporary, but the things which are not seen are eternal.
2 CORINTHIANS 4:18 NKJV

Father God, I wish I had your sight today. I wish I could see past my circumstances into eternity, where all your promises are fulfilled, where this present suffering is forgotten, and where I am happy and whole and free. To you this moment in time is an eye blink. To me, it feels like it will never end. Quiet my heart, Lord, with your comfort. Remind me this is temporary. Tell me how wonderful it's going to be when we are together. Give me a peace so profound these circumstances can't even touch me. Show me what you see in eternity so I can show it to my children.

Are you looking past the temporary to the eternal?

Connection

If one part suffers, every part suffers with it;
if one part is honored, every part rejoices with it.
1 CORINTHIANS 12:26 NIV

Ever-present God, you are over, under, around, and through all who call you Lord. This connection to you connects us to one another. Flood me with this connection, Father. I want to be overwhelmed with empathy. I know what I'm asking for. It's heavy, but it's achingly beautiful and it's as close as I've ever felt to you. Give me the joy of my son, the heartache of my daughter, and the confusion of my friend. Allow me to stand with them in complete agreement, and to meet with you there. Move me to act on their behalf, God, from this place of knowing. For as long as I can bear it, I want to feel what you feel.

Who can you empathize with today?

My Name

See, I have written your name on my hand.
Jerusalem, I always think about your walls.
ISAIAH 49:16 NCV

Lord, how am I so special to you? According to your Word, you have written my name on your hand. I remember doodling the names of crushes, of children I hoped to one day meet. To realize I delight you in this way, that I quicken your heart, is too lovely. Forgive me for when I fail to notice you. Your promise, always to remember me, never to forsake me, overwhelms me with love. I am so grateful! I would ask you for just those things if you hadn't already promised them. Never forget me, Father! Never forsake me, Lord! And then you would show me your hand, and I'd know it is written. It is done.

Do you know that you are special to the Lord?

Joy Is Medicine

A joyful heart is good medicine,
But a broken spirit dries up the bones.
PROVERBS 17:22 NASB

Lord, your joy is my strength, my source of healing, my medicine. I'm sorry for how quickly I turn to other sources, trying to fix myself without you. Doctors and their prescriptions are good, but without your joy in my heart, the health of my body doesn't count for much. Remind me, God, to seek you first. Show me how often a shift in perspective or a change in focus can heal me. Reveal to me when an ache in my body is a call to return to your fountain of joy. And when I do need physical healing, remind me how much faster it comes to a heart that's full.

How can you make joy your medicine today?

Get It Right

"Where your treasure is, there will your heart be also."
LUKE 12:34 ESV

Father, how do you manage to make every one of your children your number one priority? Even when we feel forgotten, the truth of your dedication is there. I don't even know if I could name my number one priority, and this grieves me. I sometimes feel like I just float from fire to fire, waving my hose. Oh Lord, help me get this right! Place your values prominently in me, so the flames of distraction can't so easily tear me away from what matters. Inspire me to make honoring and following you my number one priority, so I can know that whatever captures my heart and attention is what is on yours.

What is your number one priority? Where is your treasure?

Not Worried

Anxiety weighs down the human heart,
but a good word cheers it up.
PROVERBS 12:25 NRSV

Wise Father, what is it like to not know worry? I can't conceive it. All your children, whom you love so deeply, and all the perilous positions we put ourselves in—all the dangerous choices we make—it makes me glad you already know the outcome. But wait. I know it, too, don't I? Why then, when I know how the story ends, do I worry? It's like seeing a movie for the second time and expecting the story to change. All I accomplish is to produce heaviness in my heart and fear in my gut. Pointless! Help me let it go, Father, to trust the ending you've written, and enjoy the show.

Are you enjoying what God has in store for you?

Wealth of Character

Choose a good reputation over great riches;
being held in high esteem is better than silver or gold.
PROVERBS 22:1 NLT

God, when I question what's important, I look at Jesus. You could have had him raised in a palace, but instead you made him poor. You gave him to people who worked hard for everything they had. Instead of things, you gave him a wealth of character, insight, and compassion. You really aren't impressed with what we acquire, are you? So why then does it matter so much to us—to me? Why does my checkbook consume more of my thought life than my character? Set my thinking right, God, and help me desire wealth as Jesus had it. Let my word be worth more than my wallet. Make me rich with compassion and loaded with love. Help me to pass along the importance of this message to my children.

Do you choose a good reputation over great riches?

Call to Love

Do not rejoice when your enemy falls,
And do not let your heart be glad when he stumbles.
PROVERBS 24:17 NKJV

Father, your compassion never fails. Even the cries of someone who has rejected you and worked against you your whole life pierce your heart. Let it be so with mine. When I experience a little jolt of happiness when people "get what they deserve," pierce my heart with compassion. Let me see them as you do. God, may I never be thrilled at the stumbles of another, no matter what they've done—to me or to anyone. Wipe revenge from my heart. Remind me I've got my own life to live, and that my call is to love.

Do you have a heart of love toward others?

Strength Revealed

Yours, LORD, is the greatness and the power
and the glory and the majesty and the splendor,
for everything in heaven and earth is yours.
1 CHRONICLES 29:11 NIV

All-powerful God, I'm so grateful for your strength. Just to know of your unlimited capability fortifies me with courage. Displays of power in nature awe me, and to know a thunderstorm or the jaws of a lion are no match for you leaves me dumbstruck. This is the power at work in my life. Thank you, Lord. Thank you that you choose to reveal and use your strength in me and for me. The power that surges through me just from calling on your name overflows me with gratitude. The strength I receive in answer to prayer weakens my knees with awe. I need your strength today as I manage a house full of different schedules, needs, and opinions. Fill me with strength today, God.

Are you grateful for God's power that is working in your life?

The Only Judge

God is the only Lawmaker and Judge. He is the only
One who can save and destroy. So it is not right
for you to judge your neighbor.

JAMES 4:12 NCV

Lord, you are the only judge. Remind me of this, Father, as I am sinking under the weight of the opinions of others. Whether I'm being misunderstood or whether their assessment is accurate, remind me it is irrelevant. Only you get to decide who I am. Don't let the judgment of others sway, change, or hurt me, God. Let their opinions feel inconsequential to me, as they are in your eyes. If I need conviction, let it come from you and you alone. If I must stand trial, let me stand under you. Only you know my heart, Lord, and only you can change it. Everything else is noise.

Are you convinced that God is the only true judge?

Faithful in Little

"He who is faithful in a very little thing is faithful
also in much; and he who is unrighteous
in a very little thing is unrighteous also in much."
LUKE 16:10 NASB

Lord, when you give me a job to do, I'm as proud
as my children when they help me. I feel so trusted
and so valued. Like that little child, I know I don't
always do it right. I know it would be far easier to
do it yourself, but still you give me responsibility for
something that matters to you—and that matters
so much to me! Trust me more, Father. I want to be
a faithful servant with what you've entrusted to me.
Bring me to a place where I can provide, thrive, and
serve all at once. Because that's how you've taught
me, I'm dreaming big. Pick me up and place me where
I can make you proud.

How are you being faithful in the little things?

Honest Worship

Oh come, let us worship and bow down;
let us kneel before the LORD, our Maker!
PSALM 95:6 ESV

Father, show me what it means to honestly worship you. I know my efforts are lacking, halfhearted. I'm too aware of myself—how I look, how I sound—to direct all my attention to you. Can it even please you when so much of my focus remains on me? Forgive my soulless singing, my refusal to hit my knees. God, I want to forget I even exist and get lost in adoring you. Arms raised, not because the crowds are, but because I'm grasping desperately for your touch. My body swaying, not to the beat of the music, but to the beat of your heart.

Is your heart's desire to honestly worship your God?

Show Me Beauty

I praise you, for I am fearfully and wonderfully made.
Wonderful are your works; that I know very well.
PSALM 139:14 NRSV

Father, if you are perfect, and if you make no mistakes, that must mean I am exactly as you intended me to be and my children are the same. We must be lovely in your sight. Oh Father, sometimes I don't see it. I see bumps, bulges, spots, and sins. I see things that need to improve and things I'd like to remove. I may be more than acceptable to you, but I'm struggling to accept myself. I want to ask you to make me different, to change the things I don't like, but I know that what I really need is to see as you see. Show me the true beauty, Lord, through your eyes. Then help me accept what I see.

Do you know that the Lord made you wonderful?

Bold Confidence

It is not that we think we are qualified to do anything on our own. Our qualification comes from God.
2 CORINTHIANS 3:5 NLT

Creator God, what is beyond your capability? What task are you unqualified for? When I feel overwhelmed and incapable, help me remember I don't need to panic. We are in this together, and your awesomeness more than makes up for my shortcomings. When I lack confidence, let me find it in you. You wouldn't have given this task to me if I couldn't pull it off. You may allow a fair amount of struggle and strife as I go, but that's just to remind me how much I need you! Make me bold with confidence, Lord, and infuse me with your ability. If this work I do is for you, I cannot fail.

Is your confidence in your Creator?

Redemption

"As for you, you meant evil against me;
but God meant it for good, in order to bring it about
as it is this day, to save many people alive."
GENESIS 50:20 NKJV

Father, you make everything good. Even the evil in this world turns to loveliness in your hands. Just as you turned the betrayal of Joseph's brothers into prosperity for a nation, reconciliation for a family, and the saving of many lives, you can redeem the ugliest deeds imaginable still today. This is why I don't need to fear evil—because it can't stand against you. And while I wait with trembling knees and tear-swelled eyes to see how you redeem tragedy and destruction, I'm invited to take shelter under and rest in your promise. You work everything out for the good of those who love you, and I do love you.

Is there something evil against you that you can see God turning to good?

I Have Faith

Faith is confidence in what we hope for
and assurance about what we do not see.
HEBREWS 11:1 NIV

Lord, I have hopes, dreams, and goals. I know
where I'd like to end up, and what I hope will happen
along the way. I have faith that the path you've set
me on will get me there. You're in charge, God, and
this explodes me with confidence. I trust you with
my life. One day, I know I'll doubt this conviction. A
fork in the road or an unexpected storm will have me
questioning the whole journey. On that day, remind
me of this: I trust my goals because I set them with
you in my heart. I don't doubt my dreams for myself
or my children because I believe they were from you.
And my hope? I've placed it in your hands. I have
faith in you, Lord.

Do you have faith in the Lord?

Goodness Itself

Let love be genuine. Abhor what is evil;
hold fast to what is good.
ROMANS 12:9 ESV

God, you are goodness itself. To desire what is good is to desire you, and to do good is to become more and more filled with you. I can't understand my attraction to anything else. What does a show about murder, betrayal, and emptiness have to offer me when I could be meditating on the millions of ways you are wonderful? Why gossip when I can share your love? Lord, I want to hate the darkness. Give me a bitter taste when it encroaches on me. Cause me to recoil in protest. Help me cling to truth, loveliness, and light, pursuing goodness and finding you.

Is your love genuine? Do you abhor evil and hold fast to what is good?

Willing to Listen

A wise warning to someone who will listen
is as valuable as gold earrings or fine gold jewelry.
PROVERBS 25:12 NCV

Lord, thank you for the advisors and counselors you've provided as I've gone through life. You gave them wisdom and patience, and I benefit from both. You and they forgave the times I was too arrogant or stubborn to listen, and you rejoiced with them when I heard them, saving myself the trouble of another lesson learned the hard way. Thank you also for the chance to pass this blessing on, as you've placed these children in my life who are willing to listen to me. Thank you for tenderness and grace toward them as they ignore my advice. And thank you for wisdom on the days they take it to heart.

Are you willing to listen?

Better than Life

Because Your lovingkindness is better than life,
My lips will praise You.
PSALM 63:3 NASB

Lord, I praise you for your kindness. You do things that teach us, grow our faith, and advance your kingdom here on earth, but you also do things out of pure kindness. Like a gift "just because," you delight in bestowing blessings on your children. How precious these gifts are to me. In return, I offer you my sincerest praise. I celebrate your kind heart, your loving ways, and your perfect gifts. I rejoice in your attention to what delights me, and I sing of your unending love. I could sing and dance, write and pray, read and dream all day long and it wouldn't be enough to thank you. You are so very, very kind, my God. Help me to show this same kindness to my children, giving them gifts just because I love them and because they delight my heart.

How can you praise God today for his lovingkindness?

Without Regret

Godly grief produces a repentance that leads to salvation
and brings no regret, but worldly grief produces death.
2 CORINTHIANS 7:10 NRSV

Lord, one of your most unfathomable gifts is a life
without regret. The freedom must be more than most
of us can bear, because we have a terribly hard
time accepting that gift, don't we? But oh, what a
beautiful day it will be to wake up and realize regret
is gone! I have glimpses of it now. I remember an old
sin and instead of self-condemnation and shame,
I experience a few moments of peace, of gratitude
those days are behind me. Then the voice speaks up,
the one that says, how can you be happy right now?
Help me silence that voice, Lord! Let me seize your
grace and be free of regret once and for all.

Are you living a life without regret?

No More Boulders

"Build up, build up, prepare the road!
Remove the obstacles out of the way of my people."
ISAIAH 57:14 NIV

As the God who moves mountains, can I ask you to take care of this field of boulders, Lord? I'm trying to make my way, to do good, but I keep stumbling or having to alter my course. I know you will move all the obstacles if I ask with a heart set on you, so please unclutter my heart. Free it so I can continue on my way. I know you are always up to something good, but this journey is starting to wear me out. My children are struggling, and I am struggling to help. Meanwhile, the boulders. They roll in from all sides; they drop from the sky. Clear the road, Father, as you clear my heart.

What boulders do you need God to remove from your road?

Seize My Heart

Let us pursue the things which make for peace
and the things by which one may edify another.
ROMANS 14:19 NKJV

Jesus, lover of my soul, I can't believe you pursue me—that I captivate you. The thought brings me such peace, such a sense of being enough. Thank you for that. I often say I need peace—and I know I'm in love with you—but when I take a look at what I'm pursuing, it would seem to be chaos that has me captivated. Lord, seize my heart! Help me turn from the craziness of achievement and busyness and to be content simply with being adored by you. Let me rest in it; let it captivate me. Let me turn my pursuit to you, Lord, and when I catch you, may I fall into the peace of your waiting arms.

Are you pursuing things that make for peace?

Too Much

"Come to me, all who labor and are heavy laden,
and I will give you rest."
MATTHEW 11:28 ESV

Precious Lord, how can you be so kind? I know your burdens are tremendous; you hold all we cannot carry. Yet you call to me, offering to take mine on too. How beautiful you are! Jesus, I admit I am weary. My labor is long; my burden is heavy. Thank you, Lord, for your invitation. It's so like you to take my burden as your own. Thank you for your offer of rest. Where else could I find it, with so much to carry? Who else could I trust to watch over this load of motherhood while I recover my strength, and in whom could I have faith to stir me when it's time to return? Only you, gracious Lord.

What is too much for you right now that you could give to God?

Self-Control

The end of all things is near; therefore be serious
and discipline yourselves for the sake of your prayers.
1 PETER 4:7 NRSV

God, your grace and inventiveness constantly amaze me. Because of Jesus, we don't need to obey you to earn our place in heaven. But your laws exist to spare us the pain and consequences of separation from you, so we still need to discipline ourselves. You knew even under grace we'd struggle with sin, so you sent your Holy Spirit, who gives us self-control. Thank you, Lord, for the discerning power of the Holy Spirit. Please send that power now and help me control my flesh. I want to live free of the consequences of sin and remain in your presence.

Are you disciplining yourself for the end?

Accountability

As iron sharpens iron,
so a friend sharpens a friend.
PROVERBS 27:17 NLT

Father, you take care of every need, even the ones I don't know to ask for. I'm sure I'm too proud to have requested it, but having friends who hold me accountable to your standards is such a gift! Sure, it's great having people to laugh and have fun with, but it's the ones who inspire me to be a better person who really give life meaning. When I am avoiding one of these precious people, sound an alarm, Lord. Have me check my heart to see what it is I'm trying to keep hidden. Embolden me to show it to them before they ask and lead them to pray with me for the strength to let it go.

Do you have a friend that holds you accountable?

Forget Fear

He said, "Come." And when Peter had come down
out of the boat, he walked on the water to go to Jesus.
MATTHEW 14:29 NKJV

Lord, when I focus on you, I forget to be afraid. All I see is love and possibility, and fear is simply thrown away. It is when I look down and realize where I am that I begin to doubt. How did I get here? What was I thinking? This can't be done! Just like that, I start to sink. Jesus, hold my chin in your loving hand. Lock your eyes on me and tell me anything is possible. I take courage from you, Lord, and I take fear and apprehension from the world. What will I take today? Help me choose well.

Is your focus on God? Do you take courage from him?

No Despair

The righteous person may have many troubles,
but the LORD delivers him from them all.
PSALM 34:19 NIV

God, you are my deliverer! Whether I be lost, friendless, penniless, hopeless, or mired in sin, you will keep your promise and bring me home. What an awesome truth! It amazes me more every time you come for me, lifting me out of despair, and carrying me to the peace and safety of hope. Lord, come for me again—now. I'm not even sure how I got here, only that I am here, and all I see is black. Shine on me, Father, enveloping me in your light. It's lonely here and I'm full of fear, but I will not despair.

Are there troubles that you need the Lord to deliver you from?

Beyond Reason

What should we say about this? If God is for us,
no one can defeat us.
ROMANS 8:31 NCV

God, my general, my captain, my father, my friend,
as I consider all you are to me, I realize I cannot fail.
I recognize the power I have as your child, and I am
encouraged beyond all human reason. If only I could
lose my human reason entirely and rely solely on
your promises. I can—with your help. But am I brave
enough to ask? Do I have the courage to surrender
my own logic to the upside-down ways of your
kingdom? Let's find out together, Lord. Help me lay
logic aside and pick up faith! Logic says I'm losing,
but I prefer your truth. With you on my side, I cannot
be defeated. I want my children to know the power of
this promise too.

If God is for you who can defeat you?

Surrendered

Instead, you ought to say, "If the Lord wills,
we will live and also do this or that."
JAMES 4:15 NCV

Not my will but yours, God. Yours is perfect, unquestionable, divine. Mine is selfish, even on my best day. Oh Lord, when things are difficult, show me if have stepped out of your will! Ask me if I am planning my life and the lives of my children or seeking your plan. Question me, Lord, and let me answer honestly: am I surrendered to your will? Do I want it more than anything? Will I risk the familiar for the risk you are calling me to take? Will I stay inside the boat, or will I step onto the waves? If I start to follow a dream you didn't give me, block my way. Remind me who you are, God, and that all I need to plan is to follow you.

Are you planning your life or following God's plan?

Lean in Closer

He gives more grace. Therefore it says,
"God opposes the proud, but gives grace to the humble."
JAMES 4:6 ESV

Gracious God, where would I be without your endless supply of mercy and forgiveness? I know I must love your grace, because I ask for more of it every day. I grow tired of hearing myself, admitting to succumbing to the same weaknesses and nurturing the same sins. But you lean in closer, Lord. You never grow tired of my contrition. In humility, I once again admit to failure and ask for your grace. As I think it, before I can even form the words, you give it—again. Your grace restores my dignity and emboldens my resistance. Today, because of your grace, I will be strong. You're so amazing.

Do you know that as you humble yourself, God will give you more grace?

November

Devote yourselves to prayer
with an alert mind and
a thankful heart.

Colossians 4:2 NLT

There Is Hope

"You will have confidence, because there is hope;
you will be protected and take your rest in safety."
JOB 11:18 NRSV

God of hope, you take away everything set to defeat me. Your hope is safety, rest, confidence, and peace. Your hope is life. I don't know why I set my eyes on anything else, but every time I do, the world tries to convince me it is gone, or worse, it was never there at all. In my doubting, restore my hope, Lord. Because there is hope, I don't have to wish. I have no need of wondering, speculation, or even reason. Because there is hope, I am certain. Because I am certain, even without looking at the path, I can take another step. Let me communicate this hope to my children so they will also follow you without doubt.

Are you ready to take the next step?

Pray for Others

Confess your sins to each other and pray for each other so that you may be healed. The earnest prayer of a righteous person has great power and produces wonderful results.

JAMES 5:16 NLT

Compassionate Lord, thank you that our prayers are music to your ears, especially when we pray for one another. There's a peace that comes over me, despite my circumstances, when I forget my own need and turn my heart to the concerns of my children. I suspect this peace is a reflection of your joy. I want to bring you joy, Lord, and to be a blessing to all who trust me to pray for them. I want to forget myself entirely as I am swept up in compassion for someone else. Hear my prayers, God, and heal the hearts and bodies that cry out for relief. Let them know their requests have been heard, bringing them peace, as you answer my call on their behalf.

Do you know that your prayers for others have great power?

Until I Do

Certainly God has heard me;
He has attended to the voice of my prayer.
PSALM 66:19 NKJV

Lord, you are always listening, especially when I pray. I know you hear me, God, and this renews my hope. You hear my cries for help, my utterances of thanks, and my confessions of sin. You listen actively, attentively, to every word I say to you. Praise you, Lord, for your patient ear. I could learn from your example, God, and listen when you respond. I miss it sometimes, as I continue to ramble on—forgetting it's a two-way conversation. Thank you for hearing me, Father, even when you've heard it all before. And thank you for responding, even when you've said it before. Help me to be a better listener to my children so they can also be confident that you listen when they talk to you.

Do you know that God has heard you and is attending to your prayer?

Not Alone

The Lord God said, "It is not good for the man to be alone.
I will make a helper suitable for him."
GENESIS 2:18 NIV

Loving God, the first thing you did on behalf of your first child was to make another. We are not meant to be alone. We are built for relationship, with you and with one another. I'm lonely, Lord, even with children around me. Will you send relief? When I am trying to connect and getting no response, send someone who sees and understands me, someone to open their arms and say, "Me too!" Send someone to remind me I am not alone. Even when I am hiding—especially when I am hiding—send someone to my hiding place and let them draw me out. Please, God, don't let me be lonely.

Are you feeling lonely? Can you trust God to send someone to you?

Golden Rule

"Do to others what you want them to do to you.
This is the meaning of the law of Moses
and the teaching of the prophets."
MATTHEW 7:12 NCV

God, I'm so grateful you don't treat me the way I treat you! Thank you for your constancy, patience, and unconditional love. Help me to learn from that example and help me give everyone the love and respect they deserve. Especially when I am not being respected, let me honor my children all the more. This goes against my nature, God. Rudeness inspires rudeness, and defensiveness provokes attack. Change my mind! Let an unkind word bring compassion out of my heart; allow a defensive response to produce a loving one. Help me to give, as you do, what it is I hope to get.

How do you want others to treat you? Are you treating them that way?

Let Love Rule

Beyond all these things put on love,
which is the perfect bond of unity.
COLOSSIANS 3:14 NASB

Dear Father, if I had to limit you to one word, I'd choose love. Love explains everything you've ever done, and it negates all the reasons you have to reject us. To follow your example would make life so much simpler, God. I am controlled by my moods and by the actions of others. This leaves me unsteady. Lord, let love rule my heart. Love ends all arguments, all anger, all fear, and all doubting. Love begets more love. Love ends division, punishment, and competition. Love begets joy. Love defies conditions; conditions defy peace. Love steadies my heart, giving meaning to my life. Again I pray, God, let love rule in my heart and in my home.

Is love ruling your heart?

I Am Yours

"I have not come to call the righteous
but sinners to repentance."
LUKE 5:32 ESV

Lord, never let me forget how you found me; I want to keep my heart of repentance. I wasn't living a sinless life. In fact, I was dead in my sin. I might have felt a little guilt from time to time, but it was never in the form of grief over having let you down. Now that I am yours, I hate my sins. Things I didn't even notice before send me straight to your feet, asking for your forgiveness. I'm so glad you called me home, Jesus! So grateful you showed me how desperately I need you, and how indebted I am to you. Thank you for forgiving me—then and now and for the rest of my life.

Is your heart full of gratitude for all that Jesus has done for you?

Life of Blessings

"Because of your father's God, who helps you,
because of the Almighty, who blesses you with blessings
of the skies above, blessings of the deep springs below,
blessings of the breast and womb."
GENESIS 49:25 NIV

Lord, your blessings are everywhere. Help me remember, especially when I am feeling afflicted, to look around at all you have done. Thank you, God! Thank you for the light and the warmth of the sun. Thank you for all the life that springs from the ground, and the water that sustains it. Thank you for the laughter of my children and the intimacy of friendship. Thank you even for my afflictions. They remind me to turn to you and ask for your comfort. Thank you for your comfort, which puts those problems out of mind. You are so good to me, Lord. Your blessings fill my life.

Have you counted your blessings lately?

What If

"Don't be concerned about what to eat and what to drink.
Don't worry about such things."
LUKE 12:29 NLT

God, you take care of everything I need. You always have, and you always will. Forgive me for my worries. My mind can't conceive of the provision you promise, so I start to ask, what if? I'm sorry, Lord. What if I let worry die? What if I trust you to do what you say you will do? Invite me to test you, God, and see how very good you are. Let me know how to give danger, fear, and uncertainty over to you. What if I just believed you, and worry slipped away for good? Today I will only be concerned about what concerns you.

Are you worried about your needs? Do you believe God can take care of them?

Just Decide

Be on your guard; stand firm in the faith;
be courageous; be strong.
1 CORINTHIANS 16:13 NIV

God, your strength never stops amazing me. Even your restraint is powerful. You could change me completely in an instant: fortify me with bravery, strength, and enough faith to accomplish every task you've set before me. But you don't change me. You tell me to change myself. Be brave, you say. Could it be that simple? Can I just decide? Lord, you tell me to be brave, so I ask you: make me brave. You command me to be strong, so I entreat you: make me strong. You ask me to have faith, so I pray: give me faith. With your help, Lord, I decide. I am faithful, bold, and filled with strength. Let me ask for these things in the presence of my children, so they can see where all of these qualities come from.

Are you faithful, bold, and filled with strength?

The Greater Good

We know love by this, that he laid down his life for us—
and we ought to lay down our lives for one another.
1 JOHN 3:16 NRSV

Jesus, you paid the ultimate price and laid down your life for us. How can we thank you but to do the same? Yet it's hard—it's scary! I'm in awe of those who do, and I ask in gratitude for your protection over their lives. Please be with the soldiers, police, firefighters, and other servants who willingly set aside thoughts of their own safety for the greater good. For those who do it on your behalf, reward them with perfect peace and unshakable joy. Convince them of their safety, regardless of their situation. For those who sacrifice without knowing you, draw them in. Let them see how pleased you already are with their loving hearts and bring them the joy of your friendship.

Have you thanked Jesus lately for the ultimate price he paid for you?

You Remain

Jesus Christ is the same yesterday and today and forever.
HEBREWS 13:8 NASB

Precious Lord, you remain. You remain constant, faithful, forgiving, and true. Everything you are, you have always been and will always be. Praise you for your unchanging ways. Especially, Jesus, for your unchanging love. I give you so many reasons to lessen your affections for me, but you never waver. In a world that changes minute to minute— as illusions of safety and truth are shattered by news of bullets and bombs, lies and deceptions— your permanence is my rock. The world will fail me. My health will fade. My children will leave me. But you will remain.

In a world that is ever changing, isn't it good to know that God remains the same?

Let Them Choose

When the people of Israel heard about King Solomon's decision, they respected him very much. They saw he had wisdom from God to make the right decisions.
1 KINGS 3:28 NCV

Lord, is it hard to watch us make our own choices, especially when we get it wrong? I sit in what little wisdom I have, wishing I could choose the path for my children as I see them repeating my mistakes— and it nearly does me in. Just as you allow me my mistakes, help me allow them theirs! Lord, guide the choices of these children I love. Let them listen as wisdom is offered, but then give me peace as you let them choose whether or not to hear it. Remind me how I got here, through flames, and that you'll be with them in the furnace as well.

Do you ask God to help you make the right choices?

Out of Hiding

Whoever conceals his transgressions will not prosper,
but he who confesses and forsakes them will obtain mercy.
PROVERBS 28:13 ESV

Perfect Lord, I know you see. You saw my mistake, and you see here, now, as I try to hide and pretend it didn't happen. Am I funny to you, God, like a child who thinks they can't be seen because their eyes are covered? Or am I grieving you, cowering in fear and shame as if I doubt your forgiveness? Draw me out of hiding, God, and into your light. End my rehearsal of excuses for those I've failed; help me instead prepare a sincere apology. Here in my hiding place, only blame and condemnation can thrive. Out in the light, forgiveness and mercy await. Help me own this, Lord, and then help me move on.

Have you confessed and forsaken your sins and received God's mercy?

Family Matters

If someone does not know how to manage his
own household, how can he take care of God's church?
1 TIMOTHY 3:5 NRSV

Father, as one of your children, please bless and
guard and edify the holy institution of family! When it
seems we are more concerned with arguing over the
legal definition of family than investing in the health
of their own, inspire us with love. When we appear to
have forgotten that our families are our best chance
to honor you, convict us with a sense of divine
responsibility. Lord, I know family matters to you—
if it didn't, you wouldn't call yourself Father, and us
your sons and daughters. You wouldn't send your
only Son, Jesus, as bridegroom and brother. But you
do. But he is. Thank you for family.

**Are you thankful for your family? Are you thankful for
God's family?**

Celebrate Perfection

"Why do you call me good?" Jesus asked.
"Only God is truly good."
MARK 10:18 NLT

God, in the light of your perfection, my lack of it is humbling. How carelessly I toss the word around, as if a well-cooked steak or even a stunning rose could shine next to your brilliance. Even Jesus, your own Son, refused to accept the praise that belonged to you. You alone are perfect. Your power, brilliance, and faithfulness, your mercy, tenderness, creativity, and beauty know no equal. Your wisdom, will, and judgment are unmatched. I praise you, Lord. I celebrate your perfection. I sing of your goodness and I long to bathe in its light.

Are you grateful for God's perfection?

Friend of God

One who has unreliable friends soon comes to ruin,
but there is a friend who sticks closer than a brother.
PROVERBS 18:24 NIV

Lord, Father, God, Savior, of all the names I have
for you, Friend surprises me the most. Friendship is
completely voluntary, entirely reciprocal. I just can't
believe you see me this way—that I bring value to the
relationship. I can't get over the fact that you chose
me—that you choose me every day. I am a friend
of God! This means you listen to my troubles, you
hurt when I hurt, and you are happy in my joy. Even
more astonishing, it means I get to listen to you: to
discern what you love and what you hate, and to feel
alongside you. I get to be your friend. Help me to
pass along the joy of this friendship to my children.
Let them also desire to share with you and to hear
from you as their friend.

Do you know that you are a friend of God?

Thank You

Let us be thankful, because we have a kingdom
that cannot be shaken. We should worship God
in a way that pleases him with respect and fear.
HEBREWS 12:28 NCV

Thank you, God. I pray for a heart that feels those
words the moment I open my eyes each day. Thank
you for opening my eyes today. Thank you for the
possibilities stretched before me. Thank you for
chances to depend upon and glorify you as I go
along my way. Please forgive my ingratitude, Lord.
When I grumble about wanting a few extra minutes of
sleep, remind me that I have a reason to rise. When
I look upon a messy kitchen with resignation, let me
see it as the beating heart of my home, reminding me
I have a home. Come into every moment, Jesus, and
remind me I have you.

Are you truly thankful?

Always Hope

The prayer of faith will save the sick,
and the Lord will raise him up.
And if he has committed sins, he will be forgiven.
JAMES 5:15 NKJV

Lord, thank you for all the miraculous works you've done in the past; they give me the faith to ask and the hope to believe it will be done. I believe. It will be done. You are the healer: of bodies and of souls. Even where there is no hope, you offer hope. There is always hope in healing. And even when healing doesn't come, there is hope in resurrection. I surrender all to your will, knowing that what looks like an ending to me is only the beginning in your sight. Still, I ask. I pray, Lord, for healing where earthly wisdom says hope is lost. Hope is never lost where you are found.

How have you found your hope in Jesus?

Deserved Thanks

Whatever you do, whether in word or deed,
do it all in the name of the Lord Jesus,
giving thanks to God the Father through him.
COLOSSIANS 3:17 NIV

Lord, what would it look like to do everything in your name—to approach every situation with gratitude for what has been and faith in what will be? This is how it should be. How else can I look at you but with a grateful heart? There is no reasonable expectation beyond faith in what you have planned. Let me try it, God. In this moment, flood my heart with the thanks you deserve. Let it sink into every part of my soul, reminding me of the debt I owe. And as I consider what comes next, let me step out in faith and thank you for what you will do. Let my thankfulness be contagious in my home and outside of it. You deserve all the gratitude in the world.

How can you do everything in the name of the Lord?

What Better Gift

The Spirit of the LORD will rest on Him,
The spirit of wisdom and understanding,
The spirit of counsel and strength,
The spirit of knowledge and the fear of the LORD.
ISAIAH 11:2 NASB

Gracious God, what better gift could there be than your Spirit? You first sent him to Jesus and then through him, all who accept him as Savior. The help, insight, nudges, and heart changes have given me new life. Thank you, Lord, for this most precious offering of yourself. Whatever dissatisfactions I may have, I have none with your Spirit. You take all that is ugly, all that would keep me down, and you replace it with beauty, giving me wings. I'm so grateful to you, God. I love you and your Holy Spirit with all my heart.

What better gift is there than the gift of God's Spirit living in you?

In Kindness

"You gave me life and showed me kindness,
and in your providence watched over my spirit."
JOB 10:12 NIV

Father, today I thank you for your kindness. Held up to your greatness, the tenderness you show your children is more than rare. Here on earth, greatness and arrogance are far more frequent companions. Once again, I meditate on who you are, and I marvel. It makes me hate my own occasional mean-spiritedness. In the face of such sweetness from you, who are perfect in every way, who am I to show irritation or malice? What makes me so special? Forgive me, Father—and thank you that in your kindness, you already have! Please help me to deserve more of your gratuitous favor, Lord, by giving me a kinder heart.

Have you reflected on God's kindness to you lately?

Humility of Jesus

He poured water into the basin, and began to wash
the disciples' feet and to wipe them with
the towel with which He was girded.
JOHN 13:5 NASB

God, the humility of Jesus is almost incomprehensible.
The greatest person who ever lived—the only great
person to walk this earth—joyfully made himself a
servant. Thank you for this perfect example of how we
are to think of ourselves. I confess I need help in getting
there, Father. Next to our Lord, I am proud and entitled.
His poverty, homelessness, and proximity to the broken
would break me. His washing of his disciples' feet would
never cross my mind. And then, the torture, humiliation,
and rejection on behalf of the very people who killed him.
This humbles me to the core. Jesus, thank you for your
humility and your sacrifice. Thank you for teaching me
through your death the best way to live.

Do you think of yourself as a servant?

Have Mercy

Let us therefore approach the throne of grace
with boldness, so that we may receive mercy
and find grace to help in time of need.
HEBREWS 4:16 NRSV

Lord, have mercy, beginning with forgiveness for
any time I've said that regarding something trivial.
Your mercy is a precious gift, far too valuable to
be reduced to a cliché. You know my need. You are
aware of the pressure I can no longer bear in my
own life, and you are able to relieve the suffering of
those I weep for as well. I am here, God, before your
throne. I bow my head in reverence, but I come close
with the boldness of someone who belongs. I know I
am welcome here, and that you long to answer my
pleading. So, have mercy, Lord, and lighten this load.
I give my burdens to you.

**Have you found mercy and grace in your times
of need?**

Made New

Create in me a clean heart, O God,
and put a new and right spirit within me.
PSALM 51:10 NRSV

God, just to be near you is to be made new. You refresh everything you touch. Please, Father, come close! My heart has begun to darken, and my spirit is unclean. The world would leave me as I am, but you promise to wash me clean and let me start again. Even as I ask you, I feel the change taking place. The closer you come, the more darkness you drive away. Thank you, Lord! No matter how many times I need it, your renewal is always available. It's who you are, and I love you for it.

Have you experienced the refreshing renewal of a clean and right spirit?

Miracle Enough

"Will you never believe in me unless
you see miraculous signs and wonders?"
JOHN 4:48 NLT

Lord, I don't need to see you give sight to the blind,
hearing to the deaf, or mobility to the paralyzed to
know you are who you say you are. The miracle of
this changed heart is all the proof I need. Until you
got a hold of me, stories of your power were just
stories, but now they're evidence of what I know to
be true. You are God. You can do anything. May I
never take this for granted. May I never decide that
unless cancer is cured, or mountains moved that you
are not for me. May this heart, once cold and hard,
be miracle enough for me.

Do you need signs and wonders to believe in Jesus?

A Way Home

All things are of God, who has reconciled us
to Himself through Jesus Christ, and has given us
the ministry of reconciliation.

2 CORINTHIANS 5:18 NKJV

Lord, I know if it were up to you, we would never need to reconcile. I would remain in your light and honor your laws just because I love you. But you give me a choice, and I sometimes choose poorly. I ignore your love and all the wonderful things you've brought to my life and I choose sin. This creates a distance between us, and it's up to me to make it up. Thank you for giving me a way home! Because Jesus already paid the price for my sin, I need only admit them to you and ask for forgiveness, and we are reconciled. The distance is closed, and you are close.

Have you experienced the ministry of reconciliation?

Not Feeling It

Diligent hands will rule,
but laziness ends in forced labor.
PROVERBS 12:24 NIV

Lord, you are so tireless, so dedicated and diligent,
I wonder what you think of laziness. I try to imagine
a world where you needed to be "in the mood" to
protect us from evil or to answer our prayers for
healing and forgiveness. At first, it's laughable, but
ultimately, it's convicting. What right do I—who have
so much in exchange for so little—have to decide I'm
"not feeling it" today? Please forgive me, God, and
send your Spirit to motivate me. Renew my gratitude
along with my sense of duty and let me willingly tend
to the blessings and responsibilities you've entrusted
to me. Holy Spirit, refresh my joy as well, making it
my only mood.

**Are you just not feeling it? How can you draw on the
diligence of God in this time?**

Waiting for Me

You need to persevere so that when you have done
the will of God, you will receive what he has promised.
HEBREWS 10:36 NIV

Lord, this running is hard, and the course is long. Sometimes, though I see the finish line and I can feel the crown on my head, I'm not sure I can take another step. It's been so long, and I'm so tired. I start to think, it's just a crown. Defeat invites me into the shade, and I'm tempted. I need your strength. Help me persevere, Lord! Remind me why I am running and what waits for me at the end. I'm here because it's where you sent me. I'm running because it's what you told me to do. And with your help, I'll finish because you're waiting for me, and to be with you is worth a million more steps.

Are you persevering so you will receive what God has promised you?

First and True

Do not love the world or the things in the world.
If you love the world, the love of the Father is not in you.
1 JOHN 2:15 NCV

Lord, you made the world so beautiful, interesting, and exciting. You made people so unique and lovable, motherhood so rewarding, play so much fun, it's hard not to love the world. In fact, I guess you could say I'm failing. Because this is where I am, and these are the things I can see and touch and taste, I sometimes forget this is not all there is. Forgive my worldliness, Father! Please help me appreciate your creation, love my children, and enjoy meaningful work without making those things more important to me than you are. Help me respect life without fearing death, God. Please help me remember that you are my first and true love.

Is Jesus your first and true love?

December

The LORD is close to everyone
who prays to him,
to all who truly pray to him.

PSALM 145:18 NCV

Make Me Wise

How blessed is the man who finds wisdom
And the man who gains understanding.
PROVERBS 3:13 NASB

Father, you say wisdom matters most. I need help understanding how a clear and level head is more valuable than wealth, health, or meaningful work. I don't want to be like a child who wants to live on birthday cake and candy. Help me see the value of something so intangible and hard to obtain. I want to be mature in the things of heaven. Make me wise enough to understand, God. Then I'll be able to order my priorities as you would. Make me wise enough to choose love over success, spiritual health over physical wellness, and treasure in heaven over possessions on earth. Make me wise enough to seek wisdom first.

Are you seeking wisdom from God first?

Ever Brighter

We all, with unveiled face, beholding as in a mirror the glory of the Lord, are being transformed into the same image from glory to glory, just as by the Spirit of the Lord.

2 CORINTHIANS 3:18 NKJV

Lord, thank you for the beauty of transformation. Each time a life is changed by you, more of your glory enters the world and it becomes brighter and lovelier. I want my children to know how much more wonderful their lives are with you. Help me reflect your image in such a way that makes you irresistible, God. Make me unafraid to shine, bold enough to remove my veil completely. And in my boldness, let me shine ever brighter, reflecting you ever more clearly and inviting others to do the same. What a glorious, beautiful world it will be!

How are you believing God to transform you, so you will shine brighter?

Striving

"Don't work for the food that spoils.
Work for the food that stays good always and gives
eternal life. The Son of Man will give you this food,
because on him God the Father has put his power."
JOHN 6:27 NCV

Jesus, your teaching brings such clarity and perspective to my life. Thank you for that! It's so easy to get caught up in this life, chasing approval and pursuing the material. Everywhere I look, something points to a goal that ends here. Until I look up and see the only goal really worthy of all my striving. Regardless of what my work is each day, let it bring me closer to you. You sustain me, Jesus. Your approval gives meaning to my existence. It's so clear when my eyes are focused upward. Jesus, hold my gaze. Remind me to live for things that you set before me.

Are you living for the things that God has set before you?

At Your Word

It is by faith we understand that the whole world
was made by God's command so what we see
was made by something that cannot be seen.
HEBREWS 11:3 NCV

God, I can't prove you are real, but I have more faith in you than everything I can prove. I've read your Word, heard of miracles, and even felt your healing love, but I don't have physical evidence. I couldn't prove your existence in a court of law. Still, I know what I know. That's why it's called faith, right? If you wanted everyone to know, without any room for choice, I imagine you'd just come blazing out of the sky and tell us. That sounds thrilling, actually, and I hope I'm there to witness it when you do, but in the meantime, I'm choosing to take you at your word.

Have you chosen to take God at his word and believe that he is?

Leading Me

Whether you turn to the right or to the left, your ears will hear a voice behind you, saying, "This is the way; walk in it."

ISAIAH 30:21 NIV

God, I want to follow you, but you keep letting me lead. At first it's exciting, this moving ahead on nudges and intuition. But then the path diverges, and I start to wish you'd step up ahead of me and start walking. What I'm learning is that this is the time to be still and listen. If I'm attentive, I hear you. This way, you say. Turn here, you encourage. Not yet, you caution. Thank you for leading me from behind, Father, letting me make my way, but safely and in your will. The whispers are a gift: one I can accept or ignore. As you know, I've done both and one is infinitely better. So, tell me, Lord, what's next?

Are you being led by the Lord?

Free to Serve

As servants of God, live as free people,
yet do not use your freedom as a pretext for evil.
1 PETER 2:16 NRSV

God, thank you for my freedom. Thank you for having so much love for me and my family and so much faith in our ultimate destination that you let us come and go, try and fail, and live and learn as we choose. Before I was free, all I wanted was to pursue my own interests. Now that I am at liberty, I find what I most want is to be near you, to serve you. Still temptation waits. Because I am free to serve you, I am also free to serve evil. Guard my heart, Lord. Remind me how fleeting the pleasure of sin is, and how permanent the joy of being in your presence. Thank you for your freedom. I freely choose to serve you.

Are you enjoying the freedom to serve God?

Indescribable Gift

Thanks be to God for his indescribable gift!
2 CORINTHIANS 9:15 NKJV

God, though I try every day, I find I can't quite put into words what you've done for me since you came into my life. Life is just...good. The hard things are just...easier. I just feel...better. It's inadequate, I know, but the gift of your influence is sometimes beyond my power to explain. Thank you, Lord, for your indescribable gift. There is no one like you, so maybe that's why there are no words quite right to explain you. I pray that my joy is attractive enough to outshine my poor description, and that my children will invite you in and find out for themselves.

Have you thanked the Lord lately for his indescribable gift to you?

No More Sorrow

> "He will wipe every tear from their eyes,
> and there will be no more death or sorrow or crying or pain.
> All these things are gone forever."
> REVELATION 21:4 NLT

Tell me again, Abba. Tell me the story about heaven coming down to earth and how death and sadness and tears and pain will be gone forever. I love that story. I need that story, especially when grief sneaks up on me after months of silence. I will see them again. I will see them all again. Lord, I need that story when hatred too horrible to comprehend makes the headlines, and when people I love are hurting in a way I can't take away. God, I need that story as I need air to breathe. I look forward to the day it's more than just a story. In the meantime, remind me again of what is to come.

Won't it be wonderful when sorrow, crying, pain, and death are gone forever?

Hypocrisy

"You hypocrite! First, take the wood out of your own eye. Then you will see clearly to take the dust out of your friend's eye."
MATTHEW 7:5 NCV

Lord, the next time I start pointing fingers, please hold up a mirror. The moment I start making suggestions for ways my children could improve, illuminate my flaws. And please, forgive my hypocrisy, Lord. Until my own vision is clear, keep my fingers away from the eyes of my family. I know I've brought this before you before, God, and I expect I will again. It's a clever trap, and easy to fall into but once I realize I'm in it, I desperately want out. Don't let me be that person, Lord, who has everyone else so figured out I've driven them all away. Make me transparent and forgiving, not judgmental and deceived. If there's sin to be identified, let it be my own.

Have you taken the wood out of your own eye instead of inspecting those around you?

Take Me Deeper

Let us stop going over the basic teachings about Christ
again and again. Let us go on instead and become mature in
our understanding. Surely we don't need to start again with the
fundamental importance of repenting from evil deeds
and placing our faith in God.
HEBREWS 6:1 NLT

Lord, you're so wonderfully complex, always capable of surprising and teaching me. Even a verse I've read a dozen times sometimes takes on a new meaning when I'm really paying attention to your voice. If my faith were a fishing boat, we'd be rowing further and further from shore, where the big ones are. Take me deeper, Lord. Other times, I feel the boat has dropped anchor. My study is dutiful, my prayers are routine. Again, I pray: take me deeper, Lord. I don't want to be satisfied with knowing about you; I want to know you. I don't want to settle for being saved; I want to be freed. Contentment is fine, but I want to fish for joy.

Are you ready to press deeper into God?

Not Slow

The Lord is not slow about His promise, as some count slowness, but is patient toward you, not wishing for any to perish but for all to come to repentance.

2 PETER 3:9 NASB

God, I know I thank you for your patience often; it's because I would be lost without it. How many would be lost if you just decided today's the day. They had their chance. Or they didn't, because no one bothered to tell them who I was, but...oh, well. It's a scary thought, one that makes me more grateful than ever that you are so willing to wait for us. You love us all so much, Lord! You want us to have every opportunity to come to you. I'm barely willing to wait for anything. Thank you for your patience toward us and desire that all would come to know you. You, once again, are simply awesome.

What are you waiting for the Lord to do for you?

Peace on Earth

"Glory to God in the highest, and on earth peace among those
with whom he is pleased!"
LUKE 2:14 ESV

Lord, don't you get tired of your children fighting
all the time? I don't understand this world, who the
people are who love to stir up trouble. Harmony is so
much better, and peace—I can only imagine a world
where everyone gets along. And how I love imagining
it! It reminds me of what I've read of heaven, where
even the lion and the lamb are friends. Just to think
about walking down any street in the world on
any night of the year with nothing to fear takes my
breath away. I pray for peace on this earth, Father. I
honestly can't wait.

Can you take courage today, knowing that eventually
there will be peace on earth?

Plan to Please

The plans of the diligent lead surely to plenty,
But those of everyone who is hasty, surely to poverty.
PROVERBS 21:5 NKJV

God, Master Planner, what do you think of the plans your children make? Are you pleased with mine? I love planning, and I try always to pray and to listen for your leading, but I know I may be imagining it's you telling me to "go for it" when it's something I've always wanted. I want to plan to please you, God, so let me know your voice. So, I will never plan in vain, let me know if you are not behind me. I don't want to go, anyway, if you're not coming with me. If the road is not of your choosing, I'm not interested in where it leads. As much as I want this future inside my head, I want you more.

Do you think the Lord pleased with your plans?

Doing My Thing

Each one of us has a body with many parts, and these parts all have different uses. In the same way, we are many, but in Christ we are all one body. Each one is a part of that body, and each part belongs to all the other parts.
ROMANS 12:4–5 NCV

Lord, I long to see my children discover their purpose and do their thing. From making jump shots to preaching the gospel, there is really something special about a person who knows who they are and why they are here. I'm starting to figure that out for myself, God, but I welcome your guidance! I know what I am not meant to do; that much is easy to discern. There are talents you've blessed others with that are clearly not part of your plan for me. Help me laser in on that mysterious combination of talent and passion that will make my purpose known to me, Lord. I want to be out there, too, doing my thing for you.

Do you know who you are and why you are here?

Harder Tests

Do not be surprised at the fiery ordeal among you, which comes upon you for your testing, as though some strange thing were happening to you; but to the degree that you share the sufferings of Christ, keep on rejoicing, so that also at the revelation of His glory you may rejoice with exultation.

1 PETER 4:12–13 NASB

God, I've heard the more I endure now, the more I'll celebrate with you later. Considering this current trial, I am really hoping that's true. I must be doing well with my lessons, because the tests keep getting harder. I have to admit I'm starting to look forward to graduation—or winter break—or at least recess. Remind me it will all be worth it, Lord, so I can face this season boldly. Remind me I won't remember a minute of this suffering once I'm with you in heaven. Remind me how much you love me, that you will never leave me, and that on graduation day, you'll be the proudest Father there.

Are you facing this season boldly, knowing that in the end it will all be worth it?

Just That Much

God shows his love for us in that
while we were still sinners, Christ died for us.
ROMANS 5:8 ESV

Lord, I never get tired of thanking you for your sacrifice on the cross. It makes no sense, and that's the best part. We didn't deserve it then, we don't deserve it now, and we will never deserve it. You love us just that much, despite all our flaws. The fact you adore me as I am makes me want to be better! With a depth of feeling that guilt and shame could never inspire, I long to please you, to honor you, to deserve your crazy love. Because I don't have to change, I want to; I love you just that much.

Do you love the Lord so much that you want to be more like him?

Before This Moment

For every matter there is a time and judgment,
Though the misery of man increases greatly.
ECCLESIASTES 8:6 NKJV

Wise Father, how do I help someone waiting on your perfect timing when I struggle against it myself? It's so hard to tell someone to "hang in there" when I'm clinging to my own patience by my fingernails! Please give me wisdom as I help my loved ones trust your plan. Lord, direct me toward places of encouragement and hope in your Word. Silence my tongue when only my ear is needed. Inspire me, God, to be the exact support they need in this time of waiting. Remind us both you set up this timeline long before this moment, and that it ends in a place filled with promise and perfect peace.

How can you wait patiently for God's perfect timing?

Slow Down

The wise see danger ahead and avoid it,
but fools keep going and get into trouble.
PROVERBS 27:12 NCV

Lord, I've taken on far more than necessary, and a little bit more than I should. I've run ahead of you—far enough I can't hear your warnings or take shelter behind your shield. It's like I'm on a treadmill moving faster than I can sustain. Please, God, help me slow down. I crave simplicity, yet every time it's within my grasp, I sabotage it by adding just one more thing—pushing my speed back to the limit. Lord, if I am running straight into trouble and am too weak or stubborn to stop this treadmill on my own, please stop it for me. Take something away, even if I complain. I trust you, God, to simplify my life.

In what areas might you need to slow down?

Bold and Yielding

Going a little farther, he fell on the ground and prayed that, if it were possible, the hour might pass from him. And he said, "Abba, Father, all things are possible for you. Remove this cup from me. Yet not what I will, but what you will."

MARK 14:35–36 ESV

God, I reflect on the faith of Jesus. Facing unimaginable pain, he asked you for another option if possible, and then he surrendered his life to your will. Could I be that strong? Could my trust in you be so certain? Lord, like Jesus, let prayers be bold and yielding. I'm not asking you to test me or to let me prove it to myself. I'm praying to grow in trust so that I just know. I'm longing for a faith so unshakable that no trial could cause me to doubt. I'm asking for a love for you that is so deep, I don't even have to wonder.

Are you longing for an unshakable, deep faith?

Conduit of Comfort

That we may be able to comfort those
who are in any trouble, with the comfort
with which we ourselves are comforted by God.
2 CORINTHIANS 1:4 NKJV

Father, your embrace is both tender and strong. To be in your arms brings me a comfort that defies my circumstances. When I come to you as a child, like mine come to me, crawling into your lap and nuzzling into that space made just for me, I don't even have to say anything. You know what I need, and you provide it with love. Thank you, Abba. Please, Lord, make me a conduit of your comfort. Let your peace and wisdom flow through me in a way that makes my children feel safe, loved, and supported in my presence. Inhabit my embrace, God, and send your comfort straight to their hearts.

Is there someone you need to comfort?

Finishing

"I know that You can do all things,
And that no purpose of Yours can be thwarted."
JOB 42:2 NASB

Father, the Christmas season gets so busy with plans: purchases, parties, and preparations consume our culture. I get swept up in the swirl of excitement, and in the stress. Remind me, Lord, that the stress is not part of the plan! Take me back to your intention for this beautiful celebration. Help me celebrate your plan: to send a perfect sacrifice into the world so that for the rest of time, people like me could come straight to you, as I am doing now, with their needs, repentance, and praise. Thank you, God, for enacting your beautiful plan. As I move through this season of joy, may this gift be the first one on my mind.

Are you ready to celebrate this season with joy because of God's gift?

Blessed Words

A time to tear, and a time to sew;
a time to keep silence, and a time to speak.
ECCLESIASTES 3:7 ESV

God, when you speak, everything else stops. We don't want to miss a word or misunderstand a meaning. I think it's because we know it's important. You don't talk constantly, so when you do, it's time to listen! I fear it's the opposite for me. I speak far more often than necessary. Lord, give me an economy with words. Remind me to ask, before I speak, is this honest and kind? Does it need to be said? Will the words I choose build up or tear down? Make my words a blessing, God, especially to my children. And after your example, let my silence be as well.

How can you speak words of blessing to those around you?

Cannot Lose

In all these things we are more than conquerors through Him who loved us. For I am persuaded that neither death nor life, nor angels nor principalities nor powers, nor things present nor things to come, nor height nor depth, nor any other created thing, shall be able to separate us from the love of God which is in Christ Jesus our Lord.
ROMANS 8:37–39 NKJV

Wonderful Father, your love is forever. It's an awesome promise. No matter what I say or think or do, I cannot botch things so badly that you will cast me off. The day we accept your love is the day we become a permanent part of your family, a dearly loved son or daughter. It's too wonderful. Thank you for Jesus! Thank you so much for your perfect son and your perfect love, our means of adoption into the most loving family time has ever known. Thank you for promising me I cannot lose your love.

Do you believe that nothing can separate you from God's love?

Extravagant Love

A child has been born to us; God has given a son to us.
He will be responsible for leading the people.
His name will be Wonderful Counselor, Powerful God,
Father Who Lives Forever, Prince of Peace.
ISAIAH 9:6 NCV

Awesome God, your beautiful purpose awes me. Long before that night in Bethlehem, you gave your prophet Isaiah a vision of the moment we celebrate. Thank you, Lord for the intricate, patient way you orchestrated our salvation. Thank you foretelling this wonderful story, giving us proof all your promises are true. Thank you for love. Thank you for hope. Thank you for joy. Thank you for Jesus. Help me hold onto this gratitude, this love for you. Let me stay in this place of promise and hope and faith. Never let me forget how elaborately, how extravagantly you love.

Isn't it wonderful how extravagantly you are loved by God?

Vulnerable

"Today in the town of David a Savior has been born to you;
he is the Messiah, the Lord."
LUKE 2:11 NIV

Precious Jesus, the fact the Father sent you into the world just as we enter it—vulnerable, helpless, and small—awes me all the more. You came by your empathy the hard way, experiencing all the pain, temptation, and trials we do. Thank you so much, Lord! Thank you for being young once. May it soften my heart toward these young people in my life. Thank you for enduring loneliness, rejection, and loss; let this fortify my strength. Thank you for waiting through many years for your divine purpose to be fulfilled. May this inspire me with hope as I wait for mine.

Are you in awe of Jesus and thankful that he came as a baby?

Who Gives Power

"Your sandals shall be iron and bronze;
As your days, so shall your strength be."
DEUTERONOMY 33:25 NKJV

Powerful God, you promise and deliver strength and stability. I get so weak and shaky, Lord, as I face the mountain before me. Questions of capability and invitations to resignation assault me from all sides. Forgive the times I succumb to their lies, Father! God, I stand in your promise, sturdy and certain. Your strength is my own, and it is exactly enough. I continue my ascent, eyes up, focused on the One who gives power to my legs and clarity to my mind. You deliver, Lord, every time! Each step I take leaves me feeling stronger and more assured. Let me demonstrate my dependence on you to my children. Let us all walk forward together in your strength.

Do you believe that God's power is enough for you?

Fruitful and Fulfilled

Be careful how you walk, not as unwise men but as wise,
making the most of your time, because the days are evil.
EPHESIANS 5:15–16 NASB

Lord, time stretches before you in ways I cannot comprehend, yet you never waste a second. I, on the other hand, have been granted a finite number of hours and a purpose to fulfill, yet I manage to waste hours in meaningless pursuits and idleness. If you were my employer, you would have fired me long ago. Forgive me, Father, for my lack of discipline. Convict me, so I see it as a lack of gratitude and respect, when you deserve so very much of both! Expose the evil hiding in time wasters disguised as harmless entertainment. Let me be wise with my time, fruitful and fulfilled.

Are you walking as a wise person, making the most of your time?

Perfect Father

"Can a woman forget the baby she nurses? Can she feel no kindness for the child to which she gave birth? Even if she could forget her children, I will not forget you."
ISAIAH 49:15 NCV

Father, your love is so perfect! Beyond anything an earthly mother can feel, you adore me. Past every moment I think of my children, you think of me. Beyond everything a parent can forgive, you forgive me. Forgive me for being such an ungrateful child, Lord. I want to give you all the gratitude your love deserves. I want to return it with all the love I have. Humble me with the depth of your feeling for me. Remind me you are my daddy, my papa. You are Abba, the one who loves me beyond reason. Tell me again and again, until Abba becomes the sweetest word I know.

Is it hard for you to comprehend how much you are loved by the Father?

Increased Humility

Humble yourselves under the mighty power of God,
and at the right time he will lift you up in honor.
1 PETER 5:6 NLT

God, you alone are great. It's really that simple. Daily, Lord, I seem to question this. I want my plans, my timing, and my ideas to move forward. When things are not happening as I hope, or as quickly as I would like, help me to consider that you may be humbling me. As I try to rush things, impatient for my moment in the sun, increase my humility, Father. Let me learn by the perfect example of Jesus, who dedicated himself to serving others, and was tempted, tried, tested, and even tortured in every way. You humbled him utterly, then exalted him over all. I will follow Jesus' example and wait on you, God.

Have you humbled yourself, so God can lift you up?

I Praise You

"You have pain now; but I will see you again, and your hearts will rejoice, and no one will take your joy from you."
JOHN 16:22 NRSV

Father God, on the days I can't find my happiness, you send your joy. I praise you. On the days my options have run out, you send your hope. I praise you. On the days my pain is more than I can bear, you send your comfort. I praise you. On the days grief surrounds me like a fog, you send your light. I praise you. On the days loneliness overwhelms me, you send your Spirit. I praise you. Every day, Lord, I love you. I thank you. I praise you. May this gratitude be evident to my children with every waking hour.

How can you be sure to praise the Lord for everything you are going through?

Journey Together

The LORD will fulfill his purpose for me;
your steadfast love, O LORD, endures forever.
Do not forsake the work of your hands.

PSALM 138:8 ESV

Father, on the eve of a new year, I want to pause and thank you for having walked with me this past one. As I sit here and reflect on all the tears, fears, laughter, and pain; on the prayers you answered just as I requested, the ones you had a better plan for, and the ones I am waiting to see fulfilled, I am filled with wonder. You really are awesome, God. I hope I made you proud as we journeyed together, and that I progressed toward fulfilling the purpose you have for my life. Your faithfulness leaves me breathless with gratitude; your steadfast love renders me speechless. Thank you, Lord, for doing this life with me and my precious children.

How have you seen God's faithfulness this year?